THE FIRST AGE

OF THE PORTUGUESE EMBASSIES, NAVIGATIONS

AND PEREGRINATIONS TO THE ANCIENT

KINGDOMS OF CAMBAY AND BENGAL

(1500-1521)

By

RONALD BISHOP SMITH

Printed by
DECATUR PRESS, INC.
BETHESDA, MARYLAND
1969

AUTHORS FROM WHICH THIS BOOK IS COMPOSED

PREFACE

Although Vasco da Gama discovered the sea-route to India in 1497-1498, and though the Portuguese captains who followed in his wake visited the coasts of India, yet until the time of the governorship of Afonso de Albuquerque (1509-1515) the vast Indian subcontinent remained virtually inviolate to (and unviolated by) the formidable Portuguese, whose Asian interests were confined to the land of Malabar, in the extreme south of India, to the exclusion of the kings and princes of northern India. Here, along the coasts of Malabar, the Portugals possessed their forts and factories, and here in the land of pepper, the annual fleet from Portugal loaded with spices for the return voyage to Lisbon, from which city—of which I am now very well acquainted—by reason of two visits—the precious commodities of the Orient were freighted for distribution to the corners of Europe. For the Portuguese Malabar remained the school in which they learned the lessons of Asia and in Malabar the Portuguese acquired the confidence and information that enabled them to visit the lands of the vast perimeter of southern Asia during the time of the reign of King Manuel I (1495-1521) of Portugal.

In the month of November 1510 the governor of India, Afonso de Albuquerque, conquered the city of Goa from the Moslems of the Deccan and made Goa the *de facto* capital of Portuguese Asia. The ambitions of the Portugals waxed for all parts and a fixed policy was formed with regard to the principal Moslem kingdom of India, namely the Kingdom of Cambay (known to the people of India as Gujarat), which aimed at securing a Portuguese fortress at the port of Diu, at first with the permission of the king of Cambay, and afterwards by means of war. Commencing with the embassy of Tristão de Ga in 1512-1513 the desire of the Portugals to secure a fortress at Diu is the principal thread of our Cambay narrative. And though the initial Portuguese connection with the Kingdom of Cambay was accidental, being determined by the exigencies of chance, as we shall see, yet the Portugals had visited many parts of the coast of Guzerate notwithstanding, and journeyed to the interior of the kingdom, to its capital, the ancient and once renowned city of Champaner, whose name today is known only to the few and curious, who, like myself, diligence to sift the threads of the past, but which, in the first decades of the sixteenth century, was one of the great cities of the world: the seat of the kings of Cambay, the abode of their counsels, harem and lusts, and whose stout walls guarded their persons and treasures against the assaults of evil fortune. To this city of Champaner arrived Tristão de Ga, and the companions of his captivity, via Diu, Gogha and Ghandhar, as early as 1508, and, as we shall have occasion to notice, other Portugals, by different roads, and at different times, likewise had occasion to travel to the city of Champaner, and to other cities of the ancient Kingdom of Cambay in the reign of King Manuel I. We shall attempt to give a faithful account of every recorded Portuguese embassy, navigation or peregrination to the Kingdom of Cambay, save in the instance of the commercial voyage to Diu, which was so often visited, and by so many Portugals, after 1511, that I have disdained to overlook some of the later voyages.

5

On the opposite shore of India, in nearly the same latitude as that of Cambay, lay the wealthy and powerful Kingdom of Bengal, also ruled by the Moslems, which the Portuguese visited at a later period in their intercourse with the princes of India, i.e. in the time of the governorship of Lopo Soares de Albergaria (1515-1518), governor of India in succession to Afonso de Albuquerque. Notwithstanding the relatively late period of the inception of Portuguese relations with the Kingdom of Bengal, we are able to provide a full relation of the Portuguese connection with Bengal in the time of King Manuel, principally of the notable embassies of Dom João da Silveira, and of Gonçalo Tavares, the latter from a manuscript which I discovered in the Arquivo Nacional da Torre do Tombo, in Lisbon, in which his ascent of the River Ganges to the city of Gaur is described. This city of Gaur, like that of Champaner, was, in the period that we have allotted to our narrative, one of the principal cities of the world, only larger than Champaner, and like Champaner it is today a city of ruins, whose ruins extend for more than twelve miles along the Bhagirathi River, the old course of the Ganges, a few miles from the modern city of English Bazar. Notices of the former extent and glory of Gaur will be found in the pages of our Descriptions in Part II of the present work, and in the *Archaeological Survey of India: Report of a Tour in Bihar and Bengal in 1879-80 from Patna to Sunargaon* by Sir Alexander Cunningham, in Vol. XV of the said survey, Calcutta, 1882—and by perusing Sir Alexander and the *Gazetteer of the Bombay Presidency: Kaira and Panch Mahals*, Vol. III, Bombay, 1879, containing a description of the ruins of Champaner, some idea of the extent and grandeur of these lost cities may be apprehended. The city of Gaur, in particular, appears to have been an enormous city, far larger than the city of Lisbon in the early 1500s, and perhaps as great in population as either Washington or Lisbon, a thing worthy of the greatest astonishment, not merely because of the size of these modern cities, both of which I know well, but because the name of Gaur, like that of Champaner, is virtually unknown—even to the people of India—so swift is the vengeance of destructive time and fate, that these mighty derelicts have been prostrated by the hand of man and by nature, and have been allowed to sink into oblivion and ruin, the same end that awaits every man, so that I am reminded of the words of the psalmist:

> "Vanity of vanities, saith the preacher, vanity of vanities; all is vanity. What profit hath a man of all his labour which he taketh under the sun? One generation passeth away, and another generation cometh: but the earth abideth for ever."

I might be accused of wishing to disturb the dead for no end, having this imagination, being sensible that these works of mine, and those which I see around me from one day to the next, and which today stand so proud, are likewise destined to sink into the same oblivion, like those ancient cities of Gaur and Champaner, since whatever experiences generation and birth is subject to death and destruction, a doctrine that Aristotle teaches in his *Physics* and *Metaphysics*. Yet, since knowledge pertains to the intellect, which is indestructible and eternal, and what pertains to the enlightenment of the individual mind ought to be deemed worthy of the highest praise, and not in the least vain; with this end before me I have striven to relate the First Age of the Portuguese Embassies, Navigations and Peregrinations, a subject so noble and worthy to be known that I need not dwell upon it, first for Southeast Asia, and now for the Kingdoms of Cambay and Bengal, and for the other parts of northern India visited by the Portuguese in the reign of King Manuel, which has been taken as the compass (and circuit) by which these volumes are circumscribed.

RONALD BISHOP SMITH

POTOMAC, MARYLAND

SEPTEMBER 9, 1969

PART I

THE PORTUGUESE EMBASSIES, NAVIGATIONS AND VISITS

CAMBAY

CHAPTER I   SECTION 1

EARLY VISITS TO CAMBAY—1500-1503

The Portuguese encountered the Kingdom of Cambay in a variety of unusual circumstances. Witness João Machado, who Pedro Alvares Cabral carried in his fleet, and placed ashore at Melinde (in August 1500) with instructions from King Manuel to explore the interior of Africa, and in particular to find a route to the Kingdom of Ethiopia. João Machado failed to discover an entrance to Ethiopia, and having explored part of the eastern coast of Africa, passed in a *nao* of Cambay to the kingdom of the same name, while dressed in the garb of a Moor. João Machado was but one of a score of *degredados* (i.e. outlaws) dispatched by King Manuel in the fleet of Cabral as explorers with promises of great rewards. Very little, however, is known of João Machado's stay in the Kingdom of Cambay, or of the duration of his residence.

> "He remained for a time in the said Kingdom of Cambay [at Diu according to Castanheda, Livro III Capitolo XVI]; later he passed to the Kingdom of the Deccan, since he had heard our Armadas, which went by that coast, would be more readily accessible to him, and that if nothing came of this, he would be able to gain a soldier's pay with those lords of the Kingdom of the Deccan, where there were many people from the parts of Christianity." (Barros, Decada II Livro VI Capitulo IX)

It also appears from an Arabian source: "The Arabic Chronicle of the History of Kilwa" that Pedro Alvares Cabral left a total of seven *degredados* at Melinde. This same source—being an abstract of a chronicle believed to have been composed about the year 1520—but no longer extant—relates the Portuguese settled two men at Melinde (including presumably João Machado), dispatched a third man to Kilwa and sent four "Christian perverts" to Sultan Mahmud (1458-1511) of Cambay. The chronicle records these four men reached India, where they were circumcised by the lord of the country, and there embraced the religion of Islam. However no Portuguese, Italian or any European source has noticed this voyage.

In August of 1502 the Portuguese of the squadron of Vasco da Gama saw the land of India and *"een grote stadt ghenoenit Combaen—a great city called Cambay"* as related in a Dutch narrative of the second voyage of Vasco da Gama by an anonymous eye-witness. The Portuguese saw, but did not touch, and Vasco da Gama passed southward to the Malabar coast, having crossed the Arabian Sea in an unusually high arc.

8

Albuquerque, Parte II Capitulo XXIX
Barros, Decada II Livro VI Capitulo IX
Castanheda, Livro I Capitolo XXXIII; Livro II Capitolo LXXV; Livro III Capitolo XVI
Correa, Tomo I Capitulo IV—Armada de Pedraluares Cabral
Goes, Parte I Capitulo LVII
Osorio, Liber Secundus
Paesi Novamente Retrovati, Libro Secundo

BIBLIOGRAPHY

PRINTED SOURCES

1. Albuquerque, Braz de. *Comentários do Grande Afonso de Albuquerque*, Coimbra, Imprensa da Universidade, 1923.
2. Barros, João de. *Da Asia*, Vol. 4, Lisbon, 1777.
3. *Calcoen: A Dutch Narrative of the Second Voyage of Vasco da Gama*, London, 1874.
4. Castanheda, Fernão Lopes de. *História do Descobrimento & Conquista da India pelos Portugueses*, Coimbra, Imprensa da Universidade, 1924 & 1928.
5. Correa, Gaspar. *Lendas da India*, Lisbon, 1858.
6. Goes, Damião de. *Crónica do Felicissimo Rei D. Manuel*, Coimbra, Imprensa da Universidade, 1926.
7. "History of Kilwa, The," *Journal of the Royal Asiatic Society of Great Britain & Ireland*, London, 1895. Edited from an Arabic MS. by S. Arthur Strong.
8. Osorio, Jeronymo. *De Rebus Emmanuelis Regis Lusitaniae Invictissimi Virtute et Auspicio Gestis*, Lisbon, 1571.
9. "Dela Navigatione de Lisbona a Callichut de lengua Portogallese intaliana," *Paesi Novamente Retrovati*, Venice, 1507.

PUBLISHED DOCUMENTS

1. *The Italian Version of a Letter from the King of Portugal (Dom Manuel) to the King of Castile (Ferdinand)*, London, 1881. Written in 1505.

CHAPTER I   SECTION 2

THE VOYAGE OF VASCO GOMES—1506

EXTRACT OF AN UNDATED AND UNSIGNED LETTER DIRECTED TO THE KING OF PORTU-
GAL BY THE VICEROY OF INDIA, WHO, JUDGING BY THE CONTEXT OF THE LETTER, IS
DOM FRANCISCO DE ALMEIDA, THE FIRST PORTUGUESE VICEROY OF INDIA (1505-1509),
AND WHO WROTE THIS LETTER IN THE YEAR OF 1506, REFERRING TO THE VOYAGE OF
VASCO GOMES IN THE FOLLOWING WORDS:

"Vasco Gomes carried from here [from Cochin] four *naos*
of [the] Moors and I greatly urged him to carry them to
Cambay, and from Calicut, fifty or sixty *paraos* departed,
[and] they fought with him twice in which one of them
[one of the *naos* of Vasco Gomes] passed a great part of the
day, and he went about it so particularly and knew so well
what to do, that the *nao* of the Moors at no time received any
shots of the bombard or arrows, and they aver to me that he
killed of the Moors, the captain and many people [of the
attacking *paraos*] and shattered two or three *paraos*. Thus
our Lord is praised. They were well conquered and battered,
and he goes [upon his way] well honored, and likewise they
assure me that his brother proceeded in this as [a] very good
cavaleiro."

Cartas dos Vice-reis, Número 47
The Torre do Tombo, Lisbon

THE CAPTURE OF TRISTAM DE GA, BASTIAM RODRIGUES, *ET AL.*— 1508

The Portuguese waged fierce and relentless warfare against Islam. Resigning to the native princes of India the dominion of the land, the valiant Portugals wrought their will in a thousand ways at sea. All Islamic vessels were liable to seizure at sea or in port. The plunder of a thousand ships filled the Portuguese armadas with a thousand goods. Plunder gutted the Portuguese man-of-war. Plunder helped to pay the expenses of state. And plunder helped to sustain the imperial edifice of Lusitania.

The application of Portuguese naval policy in the first decade of the 16th century bore heavily upon the Kingdom of Cambay which enjoyed the advantages of an extensive foreign trade, and possessed, moreover, a numerous merchant marine sailing to all corners of the Indian Ocean. The revenues of Venice, Egypt and Cambay were adversely affected by the predatory Portugals. At last the sultan of Egypt and the king of Cambay formed a league to expel the Portuguese from India, and a large fleet was dispatched from Egypt under the command of Amir Husain. The Egyptian admiral joined forces with Malik Aiyaz, the lord of Diu, and fell in with a Portuguese fleet at Chaul in 1508. It is not our purpose to relate the operations of war which produced the death of Dom Lourenço, the Portuguese admiral, and son of the Viceroy of India, Dom Francisco de Almeida, nor of his brave companions, nor of the loss of the Portuguese flagship. We note only that Malik Aiyaz procured the Portuguese of the ship of Dom Lourenço who yet were alive, and who had sustained the fight with courage, and carried them to Diu.

The Portuguese captives were eighteen in number according to the testimony of Martin Fernandez de Figueroa, nineteen according to João de Barros and Fernão Lopes de Castanheda, twenty states Damião de Goes, twenty-four avers Gaspar Correa excessively, or even thirty according to the Additional MS. 20901 of the British Museum. Their names were Tristão de Ga, later, as we shall see, an ambassador to the court of Cambay, Bastião Rodrigues, Lourenço (or Pero) Filippe, Alvaro Lopes Barriga, Gonçalo de Tarouca, Diogo Barreto, Andre Fernandes (or Gonçalves) "and the others were men of the sea, some of them with injuries, more like death, than with the hope of life."

> "Of the said captives, the one who gained the most honor in that deed was a mariner, who served as a topman, a native of Oporto, by the name of Andre Fernandes, or Gonçalves, who being injured through a shoulder-blade by a musket, and crippled in the left hand, defended himself with the right for two and one half days from the *gávea*-crow's nest without allowing anyone to enter until Melique Az [Malik Aiyaz], seeing what a brave man he was, arranged that no one should fire at him, and with great promises, and oath for the security of his life, [induced] him to surrender." (Barros, Decada II Livro II Capitulo VIII)

The Portuguese captives were honorably treated by Malik Aiyaz. The admiral of the fleet of Egypt, Amir Husain, wished to send them to the sultan

11

of Egypt in testimony of his victory. Malik Aiyaz, however, kept them for his own purposes, and principally, as he feared the vengeance of the Viceroy, he desired the captives as a pledge against his wrath.

The Portuguese captives were carried to Diu. They were lodged at a villa five Portuguese leagues from the city,* as Gaspar Correa indicates, and were carried to the port of Gogha on the Gulf of Cambay, according to João de Barros, as we shall see.

> "Melequiaz [Malik Aiyaz] sent the captives to one [place], his villa, that he had five leagues from Diu, with a lovely orchard, and springs of water, and beautiful houses in which the captives were lodged, each one in a magnificent house with their lads, who were able to save some. There he sent them money, very liberally, for their expenses, for which servants went abroad to buy, and their lads obliged them to eat, and all with *cateres*-divans, and chamber, and appareled as would be suitable, and well-guarded. At that place Melequiaz would come to visit them on many occasions and console them for their fortune to whom he would give some excuses—that he had only gone to Chaul to protect and respond to Dom Lourenço if some evil should befall him; to which the captives did not respond save to the will which they perceived in Melequiaz [Malik Aiyaz]." (Correa, Tomo I Capitulo XVI)

Barros records that the Viceroy, Dom Francisco de Almeida, when he knew of the result of the Battle of Chaul, dispatched a Brahman (or possibly two Brahmans as we learn in a letter directed to King Manuel) from Cochin to Cambay for intelligence concerning the fate of his son. The Brahman, Barros continues, came upon the captives at Gogha, where they had arrived as prisoners in *carretas*-carts; evidently from the city of Diu. The Brahman approached a cart in the manner of a mendicant supplicating for alms, after the mode of the Gentiles of India, where he found Tristão de Ga and Bastião Rodrigues, and when he came to them he gave them a *pelouro de cêra*-ball of wax, and told them to respond to what they found inside, and that he would return in two days. Inside the wax they discovered a letter from Dom Francisco de Almeida, in which the Viceroy desired to know if his son were dead, and which men were prisoners, so that he could provide for their liberty. Tristão de Ga and Bastião Rodrigues answered the Viceroy upon the back of the letter, which was delivered to the Brahman in the wax, after the manner it had been delivered to them. When the Brahman, however, returned to the Viceroy with these answers, Dom Francisco, by many authentic proofs, knew of the death of Dom Lourenço, among which proofs was a letter from Malik Aiyaz, who wrote of the death of

---

* In the anonymous "Lembranças das Cousas da India em 1525," under the heading *Dyo e Melyquyaz e suas Rendas* we find: *Tem delRey, pera o soldo dos Remeyros que remão nas fustas, qulynar e quumque huma vyla cymquo leguoas de dyo com quynhemtas aldeas: remdem cada hum anno oyto laiques*, pgs. 34, 35.

12

Dom Lourenço, with, as Barros relates, great praises of his *cavalleria*, and of what had transpired until the time of his death.

In the same letter Malik Aiyaz related to the Viceroy how the king of Cambay had ordered the captives to be brought to him at the city of Champanel,* as the Sultan desired to see men who had done so many notable things. Malik Aiyaz assured the Viceroy that the captives would be treated with all possible consideration as His Lordship would know by the same captives.

We have the notice of Barros that the Portuguese captives, of the conserve of Tristão de Ga and Bastião Rodrigues, were destined for the city of Champaner, and the court of Sultan Mahmud (1458-1511). We have Barros and Castanheda as our sureties that the captives journeyed to Champaner. Castanheda observes that after the captives had been cured of their wounds, and had been objects exhibited to the curiosity of ambassadors from the princes of Hindustan, they were carried to the king of Cambay, and that he saw them, and was well pleased with them, and that he gave *cabayas*-Turkish tunics to all.

King Mahmud of Cambay conquered the city of Champaner from a Rajput prince, only in 1484, and the sultan of Cambay made it a royal residence. Firishta, the most famous of the Moslem historians of India (he does not deserve it), Nizam-ud-din and Sikandar bin Muhammad all relate the capture of Champaner, and in detail, after a siege of two years. The Hindus possessed the government from time immemorial, as well as a strong fort situated upon a high hill which was surrounded by a stout wall of masonry.

DESCRIPTION OF THE CITY OF CHAMPANER IN THE *MIRAT-I-SIKANDARI* OF SIKANDAR BIN MUHAMMAD COMPOSED IN THE YEAR 1611 OF OUR ERA

"The climate of Champanir was exceedingly agreeable to the Sultan, and he made it a royal residence, and founded there a grand city, and named it Muhamadabad. He built a fine *masjid* and an outer wall. Nobles and ministers, merchants and tradesmen, also built some houses for their own accommodation. In the outskirts of the city, during A.H. 890 [1485 A.D.], the Sultan formed beautiful gardens, and in a short time the city became so fine and handsome that it made the people of Gujarat [i.e. of the Kingdom of Cambay] forget Ahmadabad, and they all agreed that there was not any place like it in Gujarat, [and] probably not on the face of the whole earth. The lofty buildings of the city were inhabited by the great men of the day. Its gardens were full of flowers of various colours, and of fruits of all sorts, especially of mangoes; also grapes, pomegranates, bananas, &c. The sandal wood was so abundant in the neighbourhood that the inhabitants are said to have used it in building their houses. Now, thanks to God, Champanir is not still the same. Its

* "Champanel, Cidade de—The ruined city of Champaner in 22° 29' lat. N. and 73° 32' long. E., in the Indian district of Panch Mahals, eight leagues to the north of Baroda." (Visconde de Lagoa, *Glossário Toponimico da Antiga Historiografia Portuguesa Ultramarina*, Lisbon, 1950-1954)

buildings are in ruins, it is inhabited by the tiger, and its gardens are for the most part jungle, nor is there any sandal wood produced: its very name is unknown."

Additional Manuscript 20901 of the British Museum, Capitulo 80, Capitulo 81, Capitulo 82 & Capitulo 83
Barros, Decada II Livro II Capitulo VIII & Capitulo IX
Castanheda, Livro II Capitolo LXXX & Capitolo LXXXI
Correa, Tomo I Capitulo XVI—Armada de Tristão da Cunha
Figueroa, Titulo XXXII
Goes, Parte II Capitulo XXVI

BIBLIOGRAPHY

PRINTED SOURCES

PORTUGUESE AND SPANISH

1. Barros, João de. *Da Asia*, Vol. 3, Lisbon, 1777.
2. Castanheda, Fernão Lopes de. *História do Descobrimento & Conquista da India pelos Portugueses*, Coimbra, Imprensa da Universidade, 1924.
3. Correa, Gaspar. *Lendas da India*, Lisbon, 1858.
4. Figueroa, Martin Fernandez de. *Conquista delas Indias de Persia & Arabia que fizo la Armada del Rey Don Manuel de Portugal & delas muchas Tierras: diuersas Gentes: extrañas Riquezas & grandes batallas que alla ouo*, Salamanca, 1512. Original text photographically reproduced by James B. McKenna, *A Spaniard in the Portuguese Indies*, Harvard University Press, Cambridge, 1967.
5. Goes, Damião de. *Crónica do Felicissimo Rei D. Manuel*, Coimbra, Imprensa da Universidade, 1926.
6. "Lembranças das Cousas da India em 1525," *Subsidios para a Historia da India Portugueza*, Lisbon, 1868.

MOSLEM

1. Firishta. *Tarikh-i-Firishta*. Translated in the *History of the Rise of the Mahomedan Power in India*, London, 1829. English translation by John Briggs.
2. Nizam-ud-din. "Tabaqat-i-Akbari," *Bibliotheca Indica*, Calcutta, 1939.
3. Sikandar bin Muhammad. "Mirat-i-Sikandari," *The Local Muhammadan Dynasties. Gujarat*, London, 1886. English translation by Sir Edward Clive Bayley.

PUBLISHED DOCUMENTS

1. *Arquivo Português Oriental (Nova Edição)*, Tomo IV, Vol. I, Parte I, Bastora, 1937. This work has been poorly edited and must be used with caution.
    a) Carta dum secretário de D. Francisco de Almeida para el-rei D. Manuel—Malabar, 1508: p. 318-328. Documento n.º 43
2. "Uma Carta inédita de Valentim Fernandes," *Boletim da Biblioteca da Universidade de Coimbra*, Vol. XXIV, Coimbra, 1960.
    a) Letter of Valentim Fernandes to the merchant, Steffan Gabler, at Nuremberg—Lisbon, June 26, [1510]: p. 342-349. With German text and Portuguese translation.

MANUSCRIPTS

1. Additional Manuscript 20901 of the British Museum: upon the folio immediately preceding the first folio of the narration of this virtually unknown 16th century manuscript the following is inscribed in a poor hand of the eighteenth century:

> "Este livro se conservava sem pergaminho e com fôlhas menos no principio como está. He hua Historia do descobrimento e primeiras conquistas da India escrita na Lingua que naquelle tempo se falava, e com a má ortographia, que os portugueses seguiam. Faltam lhe os pr^{os} quatro capitulos e o nome de seu autor; mas a narraçam ainda que simples, e de estilo antigo parece sincera e he m.^{to} mais antiga que Joam de Barros e Damião de Goes e chega so ate quando Affonso de Albuquerque conquistou Goa que foy no anno de 1510 e faleceu em Dezembro de 1515."
>
> (Signed)   Freire

CHAPTER I   SECTION 4

THE VOYAGE OF DOM FRANCISCO DE ALMEIDA TO DIU, WITH THE EMBASSIES GIVEN AND RECEIVED EN ROUTE AND THE DELIVERY OF THE PORTUGUESE CAPTIVES FOLLOWING THE FAMOUS BATTLE OF DIU—1508-1509

The unfortunate Battle of Chaul was fought in March 1508.   Malik Aiyaz rightly judged that the Viceroy, Dom Francisco de Almeida, would avenge the death of Dom Lourenço his son.   The affairs of India, however, delayed the discharge of his fury.   In December of 1508 the Viceroy, however, having collected a large fleet, and having dispatched the annual spice-fleet for Portugal, departed Cananor for Diu to bring Amir Husain and Malik Aiyaz to account, and with a fleet of eighteen or nineteen vessels, and a complement of 1,200 Portuguese, and 400 Malabaris with their slaves.

The Portuguese arrived at the island of Anjediva, where the fleet watered, and received an envoy from Malik Aiyaz, Cide Alle (i.e. Sidi Ali) *o torto*, who arrived in a *zambuco* with letters from the Portuguese captives in the Kingdom of Cambay.   Malik Aiyaz sought to ingratiate himself with the Viceroy, and he offered to free the captives, apparently for a small ransom.   He also desired intelligence of the Portuguese fleet, and Barros states Cide Alle came more truly as a spy, than as an ambassador.   The Viceroy dissimulated, understanding the fear of Malik Aiyaz, and dismissed his ambassador, thanking Malik Aiyaz for his thoughtful treatment of the captives, of which the latter had written in their letters, and replied this matter of the captives would be settled in the confusion of the death of those Turks of the sultan of Egypt, whom he sought, and who were his guests.

The Viceroy, weighing anchor, and sailing along the coast, attacked the city of Dabul, and left it in ruins.   From Dabul the Portuguese coasted the island of Bombay, where the dominions of the king of Cambay commence, and entered the Mahim River Sunday, January 21st, 1509.

"And presently, a little ahead, near the entrance [of the Mahim River] are two settlements, one of the side of the north, and the other of the south, and this was larger than the other, and it possessed a beautiful wall.   The viceroy, because these were places of the king of Cambay, with whom he desired to have friendship, did not wish to attack them, and dispatched Diogo Pires [or three Captains in their *bateis* according to Barros] to those places from the mouth of the river, who, by means of money, was obliged to ask for rice, water and firewood, or to procure these by means of barter, if necessary, and Diogo Pires found the settlement of the side of the north abandoned, because the fear of our armada, and what it had done at Dabul, had induced [the people] to flee, and he went to the side of the south which likewise was abandoned: however there he found the captain [of the place] to whom he gave the message of the viceroy: and he excused himself saying that he did not have any rice but that he would send abroad for some.   And as this [reply] appeared to indicate malice to the viceroy, he went to that

place, where he found neither people or provisions, only some cows which he arranged to kill, and he saw the wall of the place, that it was wide, and had very strong portals, carved in masonry, and near it, within the place, were many buildings, principally a very great and beautiful *mezquita*-mosque with a churchyard around it after the manner of our churches, in which there were one hundred thousand *cabeceiras*-headstones. And our people going to put the cows by palm groves near by, found many houses, and *mezquitas* with many headstones and very well made inscriptions on them."
(Castanheda, Livro II Capitolo XCVII)

The Viceroy questioned some Moors who he had captured about the reason of these monuments, continues Castanheda, and they told him that at this settlement there were very ancient inscriptions (*scripturas*) which the lord of the place held in great esteem: that these inscriptions related Hercules the Great came to this land, and fought two pitched battles with a king of it, and that this place was the sepulchre of the dead of both sides, of which there were many, and from one generation to the next this place was always guarded, and held in great respect. And Senhor Castanheda declares he himself saw these same headstones when he went with Nuno da Cunha the first time he went to Diu (i.e. in 1531).

And as the Viceroy prepared to depart, the lord of that place asked to be excused for any discourtesy he had shown to the Viceroy. He dispatched twelve bundles of rice, four sheep and some oranges, declaring a plague of locusts had occasioned great sterility in the land, and what he had given, had been from his own stock. The Viceroy thanked him for his generosity, and dressed (with finery?) the Moorish messenger who brought to him these provisions. He gave to the messenger, for the lord of the land, twelve ells of *graá*-scarlet-in-grain, five of yellow satin and a red *barrete*-cap. And to the same lord he sent a letter for conveyance to the king of Cambay, the contents of which Fernão Lopes de Castanheda has not elected to reveal.

Castanheda, Figueroa, and Goes indicate the Viceroy departed directly from Bombay for Diu, but Barros records Dom Francisco, still in search of provisions, sailed to Maim (Kelve Mahim) where he found a little rice, which he distributed among the *naos* of the fleet. Here, as at Bombay, the coast was "raised with the fear of our fleet." In short the entire population had fled from the sea-littoral for the land inside: the wooden walls of Lusitania inspired terror in the breasts of all, and arriving at Diu, the Portuguese fleet fought and won the famous battle of Diu, which secured for the armadas of Portugal, and the Portuguese crown, the dominion of the Indian seas for a generation.

Having fought and destroyed the combined fleets of Amir Husain, the admiral of the sultan of Egypt, and Malik Aiyaz, the lord of Diu, on February 3rd 1509, the Viceroy Dom Francisco de Almeida with his victorious armada presaged the certain destruction of Malik Aiyaz.

"And he [the lord of Diu] found himself very much alone, without those Rumes, and without Mirocem [Amir Husain], who with the fear that Meliquiaz [Malik Aiyaz] would deliver him to the viceroy, had fled presently [on horseback Barros and Correa record] for the king of Cambay. So then,

17

Meliquiaz, with his fears, during the morning of another day, dispatched Cide Alle *o torto* to ask peace of the viceroy. And he shouted from land displaying a white banner. And João da Nova went to him and carried him to the viceroy to whom Cide Alle gave a letter from Meliquiaz, in which he excused himself for the reception he had given to the Rumes, because it was the custom of the captains and cavaliers, such as himself, to receive whosoever came to them: and that he [Malik Aiyaz] would give to him those Christians who he held as captives from the *nao* of Dom Lourenço, and henceforth he would be a loyal servant, thus of the king of Portugal, [and] as his. The viceroy, although he might have captured the city, did not wish to take it, since he wanted sufficient people to sustain both it and the fortresses of India. And furthermore he understood how the king of Cambay would certainly make war, and [by land] he did not have the forces to resist him." (Castanheda, Livro II Capitolo CI)

With these considerations in mind the Viceroy dissimulated with Malik Aiyaz, and granted to him the peace he desired. The conditions of peace were as follows:

1. He, Malik Aiyaz, was obliged to deliver the Portuguese captives at once.
2. He, Malik Aiyaz, was obliged to swear in his own law, that he would never again offer shelter to the armada of the sultan of Egypt, nor to favor his affairs.
3. He, Malik Aiyaz, was to consent that each year one thousand cruzados were to be spent for merchandise of the king of Portugal in Diu.

Castanheda relates Malik Aiyaz was obliged to deliver Amir Husain, and the Turks of his company who had fled from the wreck of the Moslem armada, and thus four galleys. Malik Aiyaz refused to deliver Amir Husain, or his Rumes, asking the Viceroy would he yield men who had sought his protection? "And the viceroy seeing he had reason approved of his decision." Gaspar Correa, who is often a very poor source, portrays the Viceroy as a monster who obliges Malik Aiyaz to burn a large body of injured Turks, and then hang their limbs from the portals of Diu. Barros, however, denies that the Viceroy asked for the Rumes, denying the propriety of this, since noble men are accustomed to protect those who seek shelter amongst them.

Having dispatched Cide Alle, and having made great honor to him, the Viceroy dispatched João da Nova to fetch the Portuguese captives (seventeen were still alive), and all came dressed in *cabayas*-Turkish tunics of silk.* And

---

* Malik Aiyaz "dressed all of them in new shirts, which he had fashioned, and *jebões*-jerkins of taffeta of colors, and draws of silk cloth, and *seruilhas*-light leather shoes for processions and black *mongis*-tunics of *chamalote*-camlet, and red *barretes*-caps because he did not have black ones, and he sent with them a Moor [Cide Alle] in a great *fusta* [to go to the Viceroy] and when they embarked he placed in the hand of each one of them fifty xarafins of gold for whatever need they might have." (Correa, Tomo I Capitulo IV)

18

in Diu, in the presence of João da Nova, Malik Aiyaz swore that he would fulfill the conditions of peace. Malik Aiyaz considered himself fortunate to be rid of the Portugals so easily, and still in possession of Diu. And yet further to please the Viceroy, Malik Aiyaz dispatched barks with provisions for all the *naos* of the fleet, and further, Barros records, he raised a public proclamation, to wit, that all foreign men-of-arms must depart from Diu, with two days grace to comply, under pain of death for failure to do so. The Viceroy concerted his departure for Cochin, leaving at Diu Tristão de Ga to load a pair of captured *naos*, with wheat and some commodities for the factories of Cochin and Cananor, and then to follow. The Viceroy departed for Cochin on the 10th day of February of 1509.

Additional Manuscript 20901, Capitulo 84, Capitulo 85, Capitulo 86, Capitulo 87 & Capitulo 88

Barros, Decada II Livro III Capitulo III, Capitulo V & Capitulo VII

Castanheda, Livro II Capitolo XCVII & Capitolo CI

Correa, Tomo I Capitulo III & Capitulo IV—Armada de Jorge de Aguiar

Figueroa, Titulo XXXII, Titulo XXXIII, Titulo XXXV & Titulo XXXVII

Goes, Parte II Capitulo XXXVIII & Capitulo XL

João de Barros and Fernão Lopes de Castanheda are judicious, diligent and careful historians of Portuguese India, who have based their histories upon the written testimony of letters, logs and journals of the prominent figures of their day. Many of these documents are no longer extant. Likewise they interviewed the prominent figures of their age. Damião de Goes, for the most part, has been content to copy from Castanheda and Barros, and as they are accurate, he is also an accurate historian, but seldom original concerning what relates to Portuguese Asia. Gaspar Correa, however, has based his history upon interviews, and although he commenced to live in India in 1514, and although he had access to the persons of many prominent figures, and gathered much information from them, their memories, many years after the event, had grown dim, and consequently, as he did not avail himself of documentary evidence to the same extent as Barros and Castanheda, his history suffers when he comes to relate events in detail, and particularly in his chronological ordering of details so that the facts are often there, as seen against Barros, Castanheda and those documents which are still extant, but the arrangement is often strangely out of order. Still, we must not disdain the history of Gaspar Correa, especially when his account agrees closely with Barros and Castanheda, since he usually writes in greater detail. And when Barros and Castanheda are silent we are obliged to gather our intelligence from him. Correa was a humble man conscious of the evils of his world. Alas! Poor Gaspar! He asks God's forgiveness for his errors, and I, with a better opportunity to see and compare implore the same.

BIBLIOGRAPHY

PRINTED SOURCES

1. Barros, João de. *Da Asia*, Vol. 3, Lisbon, 1777.
2. Castanheda, Fernão Lopes de. *História do Descobrimento & Conquista da India pelos Portugueses*, Coimbra, Imprensa da Universidade, 1924.

3. Correa, Gaspar. *Lendas da India*, Lisbon, 1858.
4. Figueroa, Martin Fernandez de. *Conquista delas Indias de Persia & Arabia que fizo la Armada del Rey Don Manuel de Portugal & delas muchas Tierras: diuersas Gentes: extrañas Riquezas & grandes Batallas que alla ouo*, Salamanca, 1512. Text reproduced by James B. McKenna, *A Spaniard in the Portuguese Indies*, Harvard University Press, Cambridge, 1967.
5. Goes, Damião de. *Crónica do Felicissimo Rei D. Manuel*, Coimbra, Imprensa da Universidade, 1926.

PUBLISHED DOCUMENTS

1. *Arquivo Português Oriental (Nova Edição)*, Tomo IV, Vol. I, Parte I, Bastora, 1937.
   a) Carta dum secretário de D. Francisco de Almeida para el-rei D. Manuel—Malabar, 1508: p. 318-328. Documento n.º 43
2. "Uma Carta inédita de Valentim Fernandes," *Boletim da Biblioteca da Universidade de Coimbra*, Vol. XXIV, Coimbra, 1960.
   a) Letter of Valentim Fernandes to the merchant, Steffan Gabler, at Nuremberg—Lisbon, June 26, [1510]: p. 342-349. With German text and Portuguese translation.

MANUSCRIPTS

1. Additional Manuscript 20901 of the British Museum.

THE WRECK OF THE *SANTA CRUZ*, THE DEATH OF DOM AFONSO DE NORONHA, AND THE CAPTURE OF BROTHER ANTONIO DO LOUREIRO, FRANCISCO PEREIRA DE BERREDO, *ET AL.*—1510

From Cochin Afonso de Albuquerque, the governor of India (1509-1515) in succession to Dom Francisco de Almeida (1505-1509), dispatched Diogo Correa, and with him Antão Nogueira, in the *nao Santa Cruz*—in January 1510— for the island of Çocotora (Socotra), with provisions for the Portuguese fortress erected by Tristão da Cunha in 1507, and to inform Dom Afonso de Noronha, his nephew, that he had been provided by the king of Portugal with the captaincy of the fortress of Cananor and that he should come. Gaspar Correa relates Diogo Correa sailed to Baticala (Bhatkal), loaded his *nao* with rice, wheat, butter and sugar, and then crossed to Socotra.

The *Santa Cruz* arrived at Socotra and Pero Ferreira, the captain of the fortress, gave the command of the *nao* to Dom Afonso to pass to India (vide also Castanheda Livro III Capitolo XIIII) in compliance with the instructions of Afonso de Albuquerque, and with him Antão Nogueira, Diogo Correa, Fernão Jacome, brother-in-law to Dom Afonso and a native of Tomar, Francisco Pereira de Berredo, Payo Correa, Black Tomas and Brother Antonio do Loureiro of the Order of São Francisco, a *religioso* of great example who had preached the Gospel in the wilds of Socotra, and many others whose names are unknown to the sources of my history.

Fernão Lopes de Castanheda and Braz de Albuquerque record Dom Afonso de Noronha departed Socotra in April of 1510, and Castanheda notes that Dom Afonso, being between the capes of Fartak and Guardafui (*Fartaq & Goardafum*) "encountered a *nao* of the Moors of Cambay from the city of Reynel." * The Portuguese captured the Moorish vessel in which they found great quantities of rich merchandise, which, as Castanheda informs, had been gathered in the course of five years of trading abroad. The Moorish captain, and the principal men of the *nao*, Castanheda continues, were transferred to the *Santa Cruz*, and from the same source we are informed that Fernão Jacome assumed the captaincy of the Moorish vessel, taking some Portuguese with him (twenty according to Correa) and both ships bending their course for India, the Moorish *nao* sailed so leisurely, and the *Santa Cruz* delaying for her, that the Indian monsoon had commenced.

From Barros and Braz de Albuquerque we read that both ships of the conserve of Dom Afonso de Noronha, being as far ahead as the Shallows of Padua,** (or as far ahead as Baticala—Castanheda), encountered a great storm, and the Moorish vessel separated from Dom Afonso, and went to wreck on the coast of the Deccan. The *Santa Cruz* ran before the storm as far as the Gulf of

---

* "Reynel, Cidade de—Rander, in 21° 31′ lat. N. and 72° 47′ long. E., on the right bank of the Tapti River in the district of Surat." (Visconde de Lagoa)

** "Padua, Baixos de—The Bank of Padua or Munyal Par in modern English cartography, in 13° lat. N. and 72° 30′ long. E., in the Indian Ocean [and] to the north of the Laccadives or Laquedivas." (Visconde de Lagoa)

Cambay and she went to wreck at a port called Nabande (according to Braz de Albuquerque), or near Çurate i.e. Surat (according to Barros), at Çurrate (according to Correa) or in front of Damão (according to Castanheda). João de Barros states the *Santa Cruz* was wrecked on the eve of the day of the Holy Ghost of 1510.

> "And as the *nao* struck bottom, D. Afonso with five or six men, as it appeared to him they could save themselves by swimming, since they were near land, they jumped into the sea with planks, and as the storm was great, and the sea ran very high, they were overwhelmed by the sea in such a manner that all were drowned, and those who remained in the *nao*, (who altogether would be fifty), waiting for low tide to come, saved themselves, and as they came to land, they were immediately imprisoned at the petition of twenty Moors who they brought with them, who were from the *nao* which they captured." (Albuquerque, Parte II Capitulo XLV)

Castanheda relates Dom Afonso plunged into the raging seas in a *boya*-buoy against the advice of the ship's company, preferring, on the contrary, the counsel of two Moors, who declared they could save him, and with Brother Antonio do Loureiro, and the two Moors, Dom Afonso de Noronha departed for land.

> "And Dom Afonso proceeded for land in the *boya*, and arriving to it, the surf, which was very great, forced him to return to the open sea, and the roll, which was even greater, overturned the *boya* upon him, and struck him in the head, and so many times that this killed him. Brother Antonio [do Loureiro], however, escaped and departed in safety. [Castanheda, it would appear, has had access to a notice or journal of Brother Antonio]. And thus Francisco Pereira, Diogo Correa and others who departed after the sea had calmed [saved themselves], and they went to land where they were imprisoned by the people of it, by command of a captain of the king of Cambay who was there at a village and was awaiting them." (Castanheda, Livro III Capitolo XIII)

The lord of the village, Miacoje (Miyan Khwaja), Castanheda continues, was the brother-in-law of the captain of the Moorish *nao*, who, as the ship struck bottom, swam for the shore and saved himself, and he related how his ship had been seized on the high seas by the Portuguese. The people of the land were greatly angered by this intelligence and desired to kill the Portuguese to a man, among whom the names of Brother Antonio do Loureiro, Francisco Pereira de Berredo, Diogo Correa, Antão Nogueira, Black Tomas and Payo Correa have been preserved of those who landed. (Barros declares Antão Nogueira drowned; but Castanheda and Correa say he was saved.)

> "And Miacoje scarcely was able to save them in a house, where he guarded them by means of his people and this for the sake of a Moor of Granada, who was there, and who had the name of Cide Alle [yet a different Moor from Cide Alle

o torto], who seeing our people, went to Miacoje, and said to him he dare not permit their deaths, nor allow them to receive any harm, since Meligupim [Malik Gopi, See Sikandar bin Muhammad, pgs. 249, 250], lord of that land and an intimate friend of the king of Cambay, would not look upon it favorably, since he traded with more than thirty *naos*, which our people would be able to take in revenge, and moreover, they would come to this place and burn it, and that he should remember what the viceroy had done at Dabul for less. And that furthermore the king of Cambay, at the request of Meligupim would order that place to be burnt, and for this reason he should not molest those captives; rather he should make honor to them." (Castanheda, Livro III Capitolo XIIII)

Since the king of Cambay and Meligupim, his Brahman Bailiff-major (*Alguazil mor*), would be pleased to know Portuguese castaways had arrived at those shores, Cide Alle informed Miacoje that he would go to Champaner to inform Meligupim. Cide Alle cautioned Miacoje to guard the Portugals with the greatest care, while at this time, Castanheda continues, the enraged people of the land proceeded to the house where the Portuguese were imprisoned, and demanded the prisoners, with menaces of fire and threats of violence. The Portuguese endured these days in agony, seeing how the people of the land worked only for their destruction. Cide Alle came to them, beckoned them to have courage, promised that he would work for their welfare, and related how he intended to go to Champaner to inform Meligupim of their captivity. Cide Alle then departed for Champaner and the court of Cambay.

The reader will again have recourse to the narrative of Braz de Albuquerque.

EXTRACT OF THE LETTER OF GOPICAISA (i.e. Malik Gopi), BAILIFF-MAJOR OF THE KING OF CAMBAY, TO AFONSO DE ALBUQUERQUE, GOVERNOR OF INDIA

Apud Braz de Albuquerque,
Comentários do Grande Afonso de Albuquerque,
Without Date

"True Friendship, as I have with my soul, Afonso de Albuquerque, Captain-major, always exalted happiness, yours is greater than that of Gopicaiça, who inhabits the city of Champaner, many times you are praised: after the proper recommendations, I inform you that your *nao* fought with a *nao* of Paverij [a man or a city?], and took it, and from that place carried it for Cochin; going thus, it encountered a storm, and your *nao* came to the coast, in a port of Guzarate [i.e. of Cambay] where it was lost, and in it came, a few more or less, sixty Portuguese men and twenty persons of the *nao* of Paverij, which they had captured, and those who came with them related these things to the people of the said port at which your *nao* came to the coast, for which reason the people of the said port desired to kill them, and as I knew of this matter, I informed the king, and obtained his mandate

23

in order for them to be brought immediately [to Champaner]; and Caixa [Kai Shah], an alcaide of Nabande, sent them in irons to the king, and I presented them to the king, and presently he ordered the removal of the irons, and he provided them with all the things necessary for their expenditure, and your people write to you, by which letters you know that it is so: and you know that in the Kingdom of Guzarate I am a true friend of yours, and things which between you and the king, of harmony, and friendship, which are necessary, I will conclude." (Albuquerque, Parte II Capitulo XLV)

Before the *Santa Cruz* was destroyed at Nabande, according to Albuquerque, or in front of Damão, intelligence of Castanheda, or at whatever place, some Guzerates had stolen the possessions of the Portuguese from the ship, as Castanheda declares, and from that reliable source we are informed the king of Cambay i.e. Mahmud (1458-1511) ordered Miacoje to collect the property of the Portuguese. The persons who had seized it, we are informed, were loaded with tortures, since they had taken much and had not bestow it upon the king of Cambay in accordance with the custom of the kingdom. The goods were collected and returned to the Portuguese when they departed from captivity.

"And so much as Miacoje collected it, he dispatched the captives to Champaner [the reader will recall that Gopicaiça (i.e. Malik Gopi) apud Braz de Albuquerque states one Caixa sent the prisoners to the king], save Francisco Pereira de Berredo who was ill, and seven others who remained with him: and Miacoje made great honor to him for the sake of the captain, his brother-in-law, who asked that he would do so, because when they were headed for shore, one, our mariner, wished to strike him with a stick, and Francisco Pereira prevented him and even thrashed the mariner, and hereafter the Moor remained his friend: and for this [reason] Miacoje made great fellowship to him. And being [the Portuguese] at that place, he obliged our people to gather some *cauacos*-wood chips from some *naos* which were being constructed for the king of Cambay, and he gave care to send the others [other people?] to Francisco Pereira. And having been captives for two months, they were carried with the others to the court of the king of Cambay, where they were until they departed from captivity." (Castanheda, Livro III Capitolo XIIII)

Albuquerque, Parte II Capitulo XXIV, Capitulo XLIV & Capitulo XLV
Barros, Decada II Livro IV Capitulo I, Capitulo II & Capitulo V
Castanheda, Livro III Capitulo V, Capitolo XIIII & Capitolo XXXV
Correa, Tomo II Capitulo IV & Capitulo XVII—Lenda de Afonso de Albuquerque
Goes, Parte III Capitulo X & Capitulo XV

BIBLIOGRAPHY

PRINTED SOURCES
PORTUGUESE

1. Albuquerque, Braz de. *Comentários do Grande Afonso de Albuquerque,* Coimbra, Imprensa da Universidade, 1923.
2. Barros, João de. *Da Asia,* Vol. 3, Lisbon, 1777.
3. Castanheda, Fernão Lopes de. *História do Descobrimento & Conquista da India pelos Portugueses,* Coimbra, Imprensa da Universidade, 1928.
4. Correa, Gaspar. *Lendas da India,* Lisbon, 1860.
5. Goes, Damião de. *Crónica do Felicissimo Rei D. Manuel,* Coimbra, Imprensa da Universidade, 1926.

MOSLEM

1. Sikandar bin Muhammad. "Mirat-i-Sikandari," *The Local Muhammadan Dynasties. Gujarat,* London, 1886. English translation by Sir Edward Clive Bayley.

PUBLISHED DOCUMENTS

1. *Cartas de Afonso de Albuquerque,* Tomo V, Lisbon, 1915.
   a) Mandado de Affonso de Albuquerque para dar ao preto Thomaz que se havia perdido na nau Santa Cruz e estava cativo em Dio, donde agora chegou, seis panos de Cambaia—April 2, 1511: p. 139.

THE EMBASSY OF THE GENTILE RESIDENT OF CANANOR—1510-
1511; AND THE EMBASSY OF GONSALO HOMEM AND ANTONIO
DO LOUREIRO—1511-1512 TERMINATED BY THE RELEASE OF THE
PORTUGUESE CAPTIVES

Between the time of the first and second captures of Goa (i.e. between
February or March and November 1510), Afonso de Albuquerque, the governor
of India, received an embassy from King Mahmud of Cambay about August-
September at the city of Cananor. The ambassador came to the fortress where
Albuquerque and his captains awaited, and the ambassador presented his *carta
de crença*-credentials, and declared the king of Cambay greatly desired peace
and concord with King Manuel of Portugal, and that, as the Portuguese had
captured his *nao*, the *Meri*, would he be pleased to return it.

The ambassador also brought news of the captivity of the Portuguese of the
Santa Cruz, and he carried a letter from the captives and the letter of Gopicaiça
(to which we referred in Section 5).

EXTRACT OF THE LETTER OF GOPICAISA (i.e. Malik Gopi), BAILIFF-MAJOR OF THE KING
OF CAMBAY, TO AFONSO DE ALBUQUERQUE, GOVERNOR OF INDIA

Apud Braz de Albuquerque,
Comentários do Grande Afonso de Albuquerque,

"There is need of a Christian man of yours, of good faith,
who you should send with security, that your *naos* will not go
damaging the sea, and stealing upon it, and we will free your
Christians immediately, and your *naos* will be able to come
and go securely to the ports of Cambay, buying and selling in
them, and all the ports of Cambay will be at your command.
And you can dispatch your man in a *nao* to the port of Surat,
and he will be able to accomplish some good thing of service
to the king, and I will present him, I will pacify, and I will
finish [these matters] with him of such a manner that the
ports of Cambay will be at your service, and you will know
that my friendship is true, and by this manner it will be
augmented." (Albuquerque, Parte II Capitulo XLV)

Afonso de Albuquerque, however, was by no means inclined to relinquish
the Lusitanian prerogative of unlimited plunder upon the high seas, a means
of revenue, and a means of coercion, especially adapted to the temperament of
the Portuguese captains (on land and on sea) and the strength of their position during the 16th century as the paramount naval force in the Indian Ocean.
Rather the governor of India proposed to strike a bargain with the Guzerates.
And as Albuquerque had the *Meri*, and one Alecão (Ali Khan), the captain of
the vessel (being a relation of the king of Cambay), the governor dispatched
a Gentile resident of Cananor to the king of Cambay, offering to exchange
Alecão for the Portuguese captives.

Fernão Lopes de Castanheda records the ambassador received instructions from Afonso de Albuquerque to carry the governor's reply to the king of Cambay, to whom the governor replied he would be pleased with his friend-ship—while asking for the captives. This embassy was dispatched in September 1510, apparently in conjunction with the ambassador of the king of Cambay.

Afonso de Albuquerque captured Goa in November of this year, for the second time, and made it the capital of Portuguese Asia. Early in 1511 Francisco Pereira and Diogo Correa came to Goa from the Kingdom of Cambay, and with them, the Gentile resident of Cananor. The king of Cambay had vainly hoped for the ransom of the captives, but Afonso de Albuquerque, in the year of 1510, had many preoccupations, with the conquest, and then the settlement of Goa, so that he did not respond to the king of Cambay, other than to offer Alecão in exchange for the captives. King Mahmud, seeing the governor did not respond in this matter of the captives, gave license to Francisco Pereira de Berredo and Diogo Correa, at the behest of Miligupim (Malik Gopi), to proceed to Afonso de Albuquerque, reasoning, I suppose, that the governor of India would be moved to ransom the others seeing two of the captives before him.

Francisco Pereira and Diogo Correa related how Miligupim had taken this matter into his hands and how they were bound by oath to return to Cambay if the governor failed to ransom the other captives.

Diogo Correa and Francisco Pereira arrived shortly before the governor departed to the conquest of the Sultanate of Malacca. Albuquerque provided Diogo Correa with the captaincy of Cananor, without regard to his oath, and as Francisco Pereira had suffered a leg injury, he was dispatched to Cananor to recuperate. Barros tells us that Albuquerque intended to expedite this business of the captives upon his return from Malacca.

> "The captives observing that Diogo Correa [and Francisco Pereira] did not return, [and] not having message by any route of their liberty, they asked Melique Gupi to persuade the King to allow another of the captives to ask the Captain-major to ransom them. To which request the King re-sponded that it appeared to him that one by one those Portuguese, by a nice mode, wished to take leave. However as Melique Gupi was [a] man very acceptable to the King, and he, [Melique Gupi], desired our friendship since the navigation of his *naos* was a matter of great importance to him, he worked so much in this, that the King gave license to Brother Antonio do Loureiro [to go] as he was [a] *Religioso*. The said Antonio promised upon his word that if the Captain-major would not dispatch him, he would [nevertheless] return to place himself in his power and in pledge of his word, he left the cord of the habit that he wore, saying that in that cord was a great part of the religion of his habit, that come what may he would return to redeem it." (Barros, Decada II Livro VII Capitulo III)

The king of Cambay was very pleased with Antonio do Loureiro and esteemed him for his prudence and virtues.*

From Gaspar Correa we gather the threads of our narrative, and Correa declares the king dispatched Antonio do Loureiro in October of 1511, apparently from Champaner, and gave to him letters for the governor of India, upon the concerts of peace and friendship, and the captives wrote to Albuquerque, and their friends, begging the governor not to forget them, that they were in danger of losing their souls, as some had already become Moors, not by compulsion, but by acquaintance with the delights of the Moors, by which they were tempted. Brother Antonio do Loureiro came in a *galueta* to Goa where the captain of the city, Diogo Mendes de Vasconcelos, and the *fidalgos*, greeted Brother Antonio, and understanding the reason of his coming, they decided to respond to the king of Cambay by dispatching an ambassador in the person of Gonçalo Homem. Diogo Mendes wrote to the king with the customary greetings and offers of service. He informed King Mahmud that Afonso de Albuquerque alone could settle the durable peace and concord which he desired, and that the governor of India had gone to Malacca, but for now he, Diogo Mendes de Vasconcelos, offered all peace and friendship to His Majesty of Cambay, and requested that the king of Cambay would be pleased to release the captives with all dispatch, so that the governor, when he returned, would find them, and therefore more readily grant peace and concord.

INSTRUMENT OF DIOGO MENDES DE VASCONCELOS
Dated Goa, 20th October 1511

"Francisco Corbinell, factor, and scriveners of your office, by this [instrument] I order that you give to the Padre, Brother Antonio, and to Gonçalo Homem, who I now send to Cambay, sixty cruzados of gold and a piece of red cloth and a piece of brocade, and ten ells of scarlet and some cuirasses of crimson velvet which I send to give—to wit—the money for their expenses and the *grãa*-scarlet-in-grain and the brocade for Miligubim [Malik Gopi] and the cuirasses and the leather shield for the king of Cambay, and the piece of cloth to give to those lords who have honored our Christians who are captives there, and for this, with the concert of your scriveners, it will be taken in account."
(*Documentação para a História das Missões do Padroado Português do Oriente, India*, Vol. I, 1511—Outubro 20 Instrument of Diogo Mendes de Vasconcelos—Goa)

With message and gifts the ambassador Gonçalo Homem and Brother Antonio do Loureiro proceeded to Cambay, where, Gaspar Correa continues,

---

* Gaspar Correa records that King Mahmud was informed by the Portuguese that Antonio do Loureiro had never touched a woman, "so that the King mocked him at times, and asked him what happened when he was placed in mind for [a] woman. He related as he never knew what that thing was, he was never placed in mind for a woman, since those things which men do not accustom themselves to, are presently put out of mind. The said reason the King esteemed greatly in his things." (Correa, Tomo II Chapter XXV)

arriving at the kingdom they discovered Sultan Mahmud had died and his son, Modafar Soltão (Sultan Muzaffar II, 1511-1526) had assumed the throne amid great fetes.

The Moslem historian, Sikandar bin Muhammad, declares that Sultan Mahmud died on the 2nd day of the month of Ramazan A.H. 917 (November 24th 1511) and that on the 7th of the month of Ramazan A.H. 917 (November 29th 1511) Sultan Muzaffar II ascended the throne of his ancestors "and according to custom distributed money, horses, and robes among the nobles, soldiers, acquaintances, and people, according to their degree." (Sikandar bin Muhammad, p. 243)

Gonçalo Homem and Antonio do Loureiro appear to have come to Ahmedabad, since Sikandar bin Muhammad states Muzaffar II arrived at Ahmedabad from Baroda on the 3rd of Ramazan A.H. 917 (November 25th 1511) and departed for Baroda a few days after the 25th of Shawal (i.e., a few days after January 16th 1512).

Melicopim (Malik Gopi) presented Gonçalo Homem and Antonio do Loureiro to King Muzaffar II of Cambay:

> "and he related to him the entire affair of the captives, doggedly asking him for their liberty for [the] royal dignity of his new reign and thus to settle this new peace. To which the King agreed to settle what he asked, and the captives [were] placed in their liberty, and he granted them license to go wherever they pleased, and he said to Melicopim that he would send them to whatever place they desired, and Melicopim distributed money and clothes to all, who were eighteen, since the others were dead or had turned Moors by reason of their vileness. Melicopim [Malik Gopi] then wrote to Meliquiaz [Malik Aiyaz], captain of Diu, to send them in a *fusta* to Goa, as he did, giving to them everything necessary for this; and Melicopim sent his letters to the captain of Goa and to the Governor, in which he gave excuses for those who had become Moors, [and] that it had been by their will." (Correa, Tomo II Capitulo XXV)

João de Barros indicates two things determined the Guzerates to release their captives: first the favorable impression which Brother Antonio do Loureiro made upon them (Barros does not specify) and second, the arrival of the disastrous news that the Portuguese had conquered Malacca, where the Guzerates conducted a lucrative trade, which intelligence greatly "moved Melique Gupi, and thus Melique Az, with fear to offend us, and to procure our friendship, since the greater part of their *fazendas*-revenues were in navigations, of which we were lords by arms and power." (Barros, Decada II Livro VII Capitulo III) The former Portuguese captives arrived at Goa early in 1512. *Finis coronat opus.*

Albuquerque, Parte II Capitulo XXIV & Capitulo XLV; Parte III Capitulo IV & Capitulo LVI

Barros, Decada II Livro IV Capitulo V; Livro V Capitulo XI; Livro VII Capitulo III

Castanheda, Livro III Capitolo XXXV, Capitolo XXXVII, Capitolo XLVI &
Capitolo XCV
Correa, Tomo II Capitulo XVII, Capitulo XXIII & Capitulo XXV—Lenda de
Afonso de Albuquerque
Goes, Parte III Capitulo X, Capitulo XV & Capitulo XXX

BIBLIOGRAPHY
Printed Sources
Portuguese

1. Albuquerque, Braz de. *Comentários do Grande Afonso de Albuquerque*, Coimbra, Imprensa da Universidade, 1923.
2. Barros, João de. *Da Asia*, Vols. 3 & 4, Lisbon, 1777.
3. Castanheda, Fernão Lopes de. *História do Descobrimento & Conquista da India pelos Portugueses*, Coimbra, Imprensa da Universidade, 1928.
4. Correa, Gaspar. *Lendas da India*, Lisbon, 1860.
5. Goes, Damião de. *Crónica do Felicissimo Rei D. Manuel*, Coimbra, Imprensa da Universidade, 1926.

Moslem

1. Sikandar bin Muhammad. "Mirat-i-Sikandari," *The Local Muhammadan Dynasties*. *Gujarat*, London, 1886. English translation by Sir Edward Clive Bayley.

Published Documents

1. *Cartas de Affonso de Albuquerque*, Tomo I, Lisbon, 1884.
    a) Carta de Affonso de Albuquerque para el-rey—Cochin, April 1, 1512: p. 55. Carta IX
2. *Documentação para a História das Missões do Padroado Português do Oriente, India*, Vol. I, Lisbon, Agência Geral das Colonias, 1947.
    a) Instrumento de Diogo Mendes de Vasconcelos—Goa, October 19, 1511: p. 132, 133.
    b) Instrumento de Diogo Mendes de Vasconcelos—Goa, October 20, 1511: p. 134, 135.

✠ ✠ ✠

DESCRIPTION OF THE EXTENT, QUANTITY AND NATURE OF THE TRADE OF THE
KINGDOM OF CAMBAY BY TOME PIRES IN THE *SUMA ORIENTAL*, COMPOSED IN 1512-1515

"So it falls that the Guzerates and those who are settled in Cambay, led by Miligobim, sail many *naos* for all the parts [of] Aden, to Ormuz, to the Kingdom of the Deccan, Goa, Bhatkal, to all the parts of Malabar, Ceylon, Bengal, Pegu, Siam, Pedir, Pacem [and] Malacca, where they carry a great deal of merchandise and return [with] others in such a manner that they make Cambay rich [and] celebrated. Cambay throws out two arms. With the right she grasps Aden and with the other Malacca as [the] principal points of navigation, and to other places in a secondary manner. . . .

"The merchants of Cambay esteem Malacca more than any other place. Anciently there were one thousand Guzerate merchants in Malacca and four or five thousand men, Guzerates of the sea, who came and went. Malacca can not live without Cambay, nor Cambay without Malacca, if they hope to be very rich and prosperous. All the clothes and things of Guzerat are of value in Malacca, since the things of Malacca are not only esteemed in this part of the world, but in other parts of the world they are desired without a doubt." (Pires, First Book)

"Each year four *naos* come from Guzerat to Malacca. The merchandise of each *nao* is valued at fifteen thousand cruzados without the least doubt.

"The merchandise which they carry [from the Kingdom of Cambay] are cloths of thirty varieties which are of value in those parts. Thus they even carry *puçho*-pachak which is [a] Root like *Rujpontuo*-rampion, and *cacho*-catechu. It is like clay. They bring rosewater [and] opium. From Cambay and Aden they bring seeds, *graōs*-scarlets-in-grain, carpets and a great deal of incense. They bring forty varieties of merchandise. . . .

"The principal merchandise which they fetch are cloves, nutmeg, mace, sandalwood, seed pearls, some porcelain [and] a little musk. They carry immense quantities of *lenho aloes De botiq*ᵃ-apothecary's lignaloes. They carry some benjamin. Finally they load [their ships] with these spices and of the other things they carry a moderate amount. And they carry, besides these articles, gold, silk and an infinity of white silk. They carry tin, a great deal of white damask, they make much over this, silk of colors and birds which come from Banda for the plumes for the Rumes, Turks and Arabians. They greatly value these at that place. They have the principal trade of Malacca." (Pires, Sixth Book)

CHAPTER I SECTION 7

THE VOYAGE OF JOAM SERRAM TO DIU—1511

In the year 1511 Diogo Mendes de Vasconcelos, captain of Goa, dispatched João Serrão, first to Cochin to load a cargo of spices, and from Cochin to Diu to exchange the spices for provisions, and "in [a] short time he returned with them, and on the return voyage he encountered Christovão de Brito, son of João de Brito, who had departed from this Kingdom [of Portugal] [in] the year of [fifteen hundred and] eleven in company with Dom Aires da Gama, brother of the Admiral Dom Vasco da Gama."

Barros, Decada II Livro VI Capitulo X

BIBLIOGRAPHY

PRINTED SOURCES

1. Barros, João de. *Da Asia*, Vol. 4, Lisbon, 1777.

CHAPTER I SECTION 8

THE VOYAGE OF ESTEVAM DE FREITAS TO DIU—1512

From the meagre intelligence of the documents listed below, we understand that one Estevão de Freitas sailed to Diu early in the year of 1512. From Diogo Correa, the captain of Cananor, we learn that his purpose was to carry merchandise, and, moreover, to know if the king of Cambay were dead and the state of the captives lost in the wreck of Dom Afonso de Noronha. And from Afonso de Albuquerque, the governor of India, we learn that Estevão de Freitas went and came in this same year.

BIBLIOGRAPHY

PUBLISHED DOCUMENTS

1. *Cartas de Affonso de Albuquerque*, Tomo I, Lisbon, 1884.
    a) Carta de Affonso de Albuquerque para el-rey—December 16, 1512: p. 382. Carta CIV
2. *Cartas de Afonso de Albuquerque*, Tomo VII, Lisbon, 1935.
    a) Instrumento de Diogo Correa—January 13, 1512: p. 8, 9.

THE EMBASSY OF TRISTAM DE GA—1512-1513

When the Portuguese captives, lost in the wreck of Dom Afonso de Noronha, returned to Goa they carried in their company an ambassador of Sultan Muzaffar II. The alarming news that the Portuguese had captured Malacca gave urgency to the Guzerate need of accommodating the Portuguese, who, having taken Goa, Ormuz and Malacca by main force, threatened to devour the entire marine of Cambay. Later Malik Aiyaz dispatched his ambassador to Goa, in November of 1512, with a *nao* loaded with provisions and to congratulate Afonso de Albuquerque upon his recent victories. And thus arrived a messenger of the king of Cambay to give greater dispatch to the concord of peace sought by his master. Albuquerque detained the ambassador of Sultan Muzaffar for some months until he had concerted measures to sail to the Red Sea and to capture the port of Aden, and this because he did not want the Moors to know he was preparing a great armament for use in those parts, and because he entertained the thought of sailing to a port of Cambay and arranging the substance of peace and concord with the king of Cambay in person.

EXTRACT OF THE LETTER OF AFONSO DE ALBUQUERQUE TO THE KING D. MANUEL

Dated Cananor, 4th December 1513

"And thus presently I dispatched the messenger of the King of Cambay, who came to me with letters, after his ambassador had been dispatched upon the peace and concord which he asks; and since my intention was to go in person to this business, and my nephew Dom Garcia {de Noronha] by reason of the great occupation which he had at Cochin with the *naos* of cargo, could not immediately come, for he had to finish these things in person, I determined, so that I would not lose the navigation for the Strait of Meca, to go there, having the intention to proceed to Cambay upon departing from the strait after the King of Cambay had been informed of the determination of Your Highness [with the] appointments and conditions with which you will bestow secure peace. I dispatched Tristão de Ga, and João Gomes for scrivener, and his messenger; and of all that he should accomplish upon this matter, he carried in my appointments and instruction, as I have said [in another letter?]. I sent to the King the present which Your Highness sent to Timoja [a pirate of Onor], and some other things which I had, and they departed in a *nao* of Meliquiaz [Malik Aiyaz] which came there [to Goa] with provisions and his messenger with letters for me, and to visit me after my arrival from Malacca.

"To the messenger of the King of Cambay and to the messenger of Miliquiaz I showed the villa which the Moors had made in Benastarym, [*] and the bulwarks on the sea,

---

* "Benestari, povoação de—Banastari, eastwards and in the vicinity of the Island of Goa, in 15° 29′ lat. N. and 74° 01′ long. E."   (Visconde de Lagoa)

and its great artillery, and the suburb which was [a] greater settlement than the villa, and the stables for your horses in Goa, and the coverings which are newly made, and two hundred crossbowmen and two hundred musketeers, because I obliged every married or single man to have a crossbow or musket, thus for Goa as for [the] Armada, as for whatever place or thing it might profit to succor; and in this place I arranged to have this body in order, more than anywhere else, since the men of Goa eat *pam de trygo*-wheat bread and meat and very good fish in great abundance, and they have [the] color of men; and they were shown how the *naos* of Your Highness grappled with the bulwarks and their great artillery and [how] they gained them, since by this display it appears to me that Miliquiaz will have little confidence in his [bulwarks] if he should make some error." *
(*Cartas de Affonso de Albuquerque*, Tomo I, Carta XLI 1513-Dezembro 4   Letter of Afonso de Albuquerque to the King—Cananor)

Braz de Albuquerque declares Afonso de Albuquerque, his father, instructed Tristão de Ga to ask for a fortress at Diu, where the people and property of the king of Portugal would find security, and he instructed him to ask the king to oblige his merchants to carry their goods to Goa, and not to other parts, since at Goa they would find all the merchandise they sought, and he instructed Tristão de Ga to ask the king to allow neither Rume or Turk to gather in his kingdom since they were capital enemies of the Portuguese.

Tristão de Ga and João Gomes departed from Goa in the *nao* of Malik Aiyaz for the Kingdom of Cambay on December 15th 1512.   Of the embassy of Tristão de Ga, and its results, we shall speak presently.

Afonso de Albuquerque, meanwhile, had departed from India for Aden and the Red Sea with a fleet of 19 or 20 vessels and 2,500 men in February of 1513.   This great armada crossed the Arabian Sea, touching at Socotra, assaulted Aden in March, but failed to conquer her walls, and entering the Red Sea, experienced contrary winds which impeded the progress of the fleet to Jidda and Suez.   At Kamaran, where the fleet wintered until July, many Portugals sickened and died from the unsalubrity of the climate.   Finally, to the tune of these disasters, Albuquerque and fleet departed for India on August 4th 1513 from Aden.

---

* Gaspar Correa records Cide Alle *o torto* came to Albuquerque as the messenger of Malik Aiyaz and comments the governor "arranged to outfit a *cossolete do almazem*-armored breast piece from the magazine and ordered a gun fired at his chest, with a ball of wax placed in paper, which gave such a blow that the Moor thought he was dead, and the Governor told him to carry those arms to Meliquiaz, so that he might see a gun could not penetrate them, as he had seen himself." (Correa, Tomo II Capitulo XXXIX)

34

Dated Cananor, 4th December 1513

"On the 4th day of August all of us departed in front of Aden and we came to view Cape Guardafui, and from that place we came in view of Divlcimdy, [*] and running along the coast we came to Mamgalor [**] and to Cimunate, [***] ports of Cambay, and from there to Diu, port of Miliquiaz, where we corrected our *batés*, and we were well received by Miliquiaz and well caressed with gifts and provisions and very well welcomed; and I arranged to disembark spices and copper of Your Highness and I left for factor of that merchandise Fernão Martins Evangelho, and [for] scrivener Jorge Correa; and having spent that merchandise, they were obliged to come; and I left the *Enxobregas* unloading the merchandise and taking others." (*Cartas de Affonso de Albuquerque*, Tomo I, Carta XLI 1513-Dezembro 4 Letter of Afonso de Albuquerque to the King—Cananor)

Fernão Lopes de Castanheda and João de Barros are considerably more effusive than Afonso de Albuquerque about the visit of the latter to Diu. The former observes that the governor intended to seize Diu by surprise, but that two vessels of his fleet, captains Simão Velho and Jeronimo de Sousa, contrary to instructions, hove in sight of Diu before the main-body of the fleet arrived, so that the Portuguese lost the element of surprise. Malik Aiyaz, we are informed, was at a villa two leagues from Diu with all his men-of-arms, when by means of smoke signals he was apprised of the arrival of Portuguese vessels, and when the governor arrived with the main-body of the fleet, Malik Aiyaz had flooded the city with his people, and concerted the defenses of Diu for the reception of Afonso de Albuquerque, either in war or in peace. The governor abandoned the projected attack, imprisoned the two captains beneath the deck of his ship, and when his wrath had subsided, restored both captains to liberty and the command of their vessels.

---

* "Diulcindi, reino de—[An] ancient Indian Kingdom which included, in all or in part, the modern division of Sind, in 25° lat. N. and 68° long. E." (Visconde de Lagoa)

** "Mangalor, porto de—Mangrol or Mungrole, in 21° 08′ lat. N. and 70° 15′ long. E. in the Region of Sorath in the Peninsula of Kathiawar." (Visconde de Lagoa)

*** Somnath Pattan? This port has not been identified by Visconde de Lagoa

✠ ✠ ✠

João de Barros, noting Albuquerque's departure from Aden, declares the Portuguese fleet came in view of the mouth of the Indus on August 16th, and that passing ahead, the pilot of Afonso de Albuquerque, trying to double Cabo de Jaquete (Jakad or Dwarka) found himself behind it, i.e. in the Gulf of Kutch while the rest of the fleet passed in front. (Barros, Decada II Livro VIII Capitulo V)

Both Barros and Castanheda relate how some Portugals (we are not given their names) disembarked to observe the disposition of Diu, and that they were feasted by Malik Aiyaz, and were shown his fortifications and artillery and in general the strength of his position. Malik Aiyaz knew how to serve Afonso de Albuquerque.

Castanheda further notes that Afonso de Albuquerque charged one Andrade, a New Christian (i.e. a Jew converted to Christianity), to make a supply of biscuit at Diu. After the departure of the governor Andrade formed a connection with a Moorish woman and fled with her to the interior of the kingdom, and the governor did not have his supply of biscuit. Of the peregrination of Andrade, of where he went, of what he did, or of what transpired with him, my sources are quite oblivious.

Finally both Barros and Castanheda note how Malik Aiyaz came with one hundred rowing-vessels to the flagship of Afonso de Albuquerque as the governor departed from Diu, and how courtesies were exchanged between them, each from his ship, according to Barros and Goes, or in the flagship of the governor according to Castanheda and Correa. And thus Albuquerque departed from Diu for Chaul.

EXTRACT OF THE LETTER OF AFONSO DE ALBUQUERQUE TO THE KING D. MANUEL

Dated Cananor, 4th December 1513

"Arriving at Chaul, we found the ambassador of the King of Cambay, and Tristão de Ga, and João Gomes his scrivener, who I had sent there upon the appointments and concert of peace. They gave to me the letters of the King of Cambay and the reply to the appointments of the peace and settlement of [a] factory in his land, and the letters of Miligupy [Malik Gopi], who Your Highness already knows by fame, [a] principal man of his land, who desires to serve you. He conceded [a] fortress and site for [a] factory in Diu, so that you will be able to spend each year in his land forty thousand quintals of copper for the price which for twenty years it has in this place, that is ninety xerafins the bahar, which in the old weight is five quintals, and all the other merchandise from these parts that they will be able to consume in their Kingdom, and for Your Highness [you may have] all the things of their land you wish. And he sent to say that I would be pleased to dispatch the *nao Meri* which I had placed in the River of Cochin, corrected again, and concerted for dispatch to him. He sent me a horse and some caparisons of metal and a dagger of his person and a saddle: and he sent a dagger of gold for Your Highness. Tristão de Ga, [the] messenger who I sent to him, was well received and welcomed by him, and well treated, and received reward. Tristão de Ga found him near the extremity of the Kingdom of Mamdaao [i.e. the Kingdom of Malwa], in war with [a] great encampment of horse and many people and artillery and all [the] pomp of war.

36

"In the letter of the King of Cambay these things are not stated, he only said he would do whatever I asked, referring me to the letter of Miligupy, who more widely wrote to me all, in which came all these declarations that I have mentioned above, and thus Tristão de Ga brought [the] same in reply to his instruction, saying to me moreover, that he [the king of Cambay] desired to have an *estamte*-lodge of the Guzerates at Malacca, and that their *naos* would be able to navigate there securely. They came to speak upon Maim [Mahim] and upon the island that lies in the canal of Gogha, which they desired to give foremost. Tristão de Ga declared that Maim was a long way from [the city of] Cambay, and that it would make the merchandise cost more. The King said he would give the Island with good will, but that it was not profitable for our *naos*, since it was an island in which there were many snakes and vermin, and that I should arrange to see it first, and if I liked it, then I should take it, and for these reasons it was not populated, and that in Diu we would be able to have [a] settlement and fortress, [and] that the Rumes would not be sheltered in his land. I responded to his letters from Chaul with thanks, saying to him how Your Highness, for the love and friendship and trade which you desired to have with him, had never ordered to make war against his land, nor to burn his ports and places, nor to fire cannon balls at his fortresses; and if the *naos* and people of his land had received some damage they were to blame, since in the seas and ports of the Kings with whom Your Highness has war, their *naos* and people are wont to assist our enemies with their artillery and their arms, as they did at Aden and at Malacca and in many other places, but the sea by their land and their ports until this very day has never been violated or entered; and other words suited to the case and time. To Miligupy I wrote more particularly, thanking him from the part of Your Highness to have pleasure to work so diligently for the things of your service, putting before him some hope for reward of his services, so as to provide for the things of your service. The Ambassador dispatched the letters to the King, and came with me to fetch the *nao Meri*, and I, to give order to the establishment of the settlement and fortress in Diu." (*Cartas de Affonso de Albuquerque*, Tomo I, Carta XLI 1513—Dezembro 4 Letter of Afonso de Albuquerque to the King—Cananor)

We shall now pause in the course of our Portuguese narrative to observe in what manner King Muzaffar II conducted the affairs of the Kingdom of Cambay between December 15th 1512, when Tristão de Ga departed from Goa accredited to his court, and August-September of 1513, when Afonso de Albuquerque returned to India from the Red Sea and discovered Tristão de Ga at the port of Chaul. We shall note how Sultan Muzaffar II engaged in warfare against the Kingdom of Malwa, and during the course of his operations on the confines of Malwa, or in Malwa, greeted Tristão de Ga, and received his embassy, according to Portuguese history, and in realizing our purposes we are obliged to have recourse to Moslem history, and in particular to the "Mirat-i-Sikandari" of Sikandar bin Muhammad, to ascertain where King Muzaffar II greeted Tristão de Ga. Let us begin.

From Sikandar bin Muhammad we are informed that one Muhammad (also called Sahib Khan by Firishta) unsuccessfully contested the throne of the Sultanate of Malwa, and being defeated by Sultan Mahmud II (1511-1531) of Malwa, fled to Cambay (early in 1512; or late in 1511). Muhammad received pledges of support from King Muzaffar II who promised Muhammad, that terminating the rainy season, he would march on Mandu, the capital of Malwa, and divide the kingdom equally between Muhammad and Mahmud. However, Sultan Muzaffar II became estranged from Muhammad after a riot provoked by Muhammad against Mirza Ibrahim (or Yadgar Beg, according to Firishta and Nizam-ud-din), an envoy from Ismael Shah (1502-1524) of Persia, accredited to the court of Cambay, and received in audience by King Muzaffar II in January of 1512.

Muhammad eventually returned to Malwa where he was defeated in battle by a Hindu, Medini Rao, who had assumed command of Sultan Mahmud's army, and not only the armed forces, but the entire affairs of the kingdom, leaving Sultan Mahmud II with the title of king. The Mussulmen were oppressed and the Hindus elevated to high position.

> "These things were reported to Sultan Muzaffar. He was told that after an interval of many years the supremacy of the infidels had been restored in Malwah, and that nothing was left to Sultan Mahmud of all his kingdom but the mere name of royalty, and it seemed likely that this also would soon be put on one side. The Sultan writhed at the relation, and deemed it a duty incumbent upon him to put down the wretched infidels." (Sikandar bin Muhammad, p. 248)

As a consequence King Muzaffar II departed from Muhamadabad (Champaner) in the month of Shawal A.H. 918 (December 1512-January 1513) with a large army to overthrow the Hindus and to succor the Mussulmen of Malwa. He came to the town of Godhra where he halted for a few days to allow his forces to gather from all parts of the kingdom. While at Godhra the sultan was informed that the raja of Idar had revolted, and had thrown into confusion the surrounding country. Ain-ul-Mulk, the governor of Pattan, ravaged the territories of the raja, but then was defeated in battle near Idar, and obliged to retire to Pattan.

When Sultan Muzaffar heard of these tidings, he marched from Godhra to Idar. Arriving at Modasa, the king dispatched forces against the raja, who thereupon fled to the hill country. Sultan Muzaffar destroyed the houses, gardens and temples of Idar; forgave the raja, at the intercession of Malik Gopi (the Hindu minister to whom the reader has been introduced), and returned to Godhra to prosecute his campaign in Malwa against the forces of Medini Rao.

From Godhra the sultan marched to Dohad where he ordered a fort to be erected. From Dohad the sultan proceeded through the difficult pass of Deolah in the territory of Malwa. Here he rested for three days and established an encampment. He knew now that Sultan Mahmud and Medini Rao had gone towards Chanderi. Sultan Muzaffar however procrastinated, and being informed in glowing terms of the buildings of the deer-park of Dhar, the ancient capital of Malwa, Sultan Muzaffar visited Dhar with a cavalry escort, and one hundred and fifty elephants, where he stayed for three days, and returned to camp. Sultan Muzaffar then terminated the campaign, for no very apparent reason, judging from the Moslem sources which I have before me. He accomplished nothing against his Hindu adversaries.

Tristão de Ga visited Sultan Muzaffar II at the common extremities of the Kingdoms of Malwa and Cambay, being the intelligence of Afonso de Albuquerque, João de Barros and Fernão Lopes de Castanheda. Braz de Albuquerque declares Tristão de Ga arrived at Chaul two days before Afonso de Albuquerque, and that Tristão de Ga had rendered his embassy at Champaner, whereupon arrival at the Kingdom of Cambay, he had awaited the return of the king from Malwa. But Albuquerque, the son, is contradicted by the superior testimony of Barros, Castanheda, and not least of all by Albuquerque the father, who declares Tristão de Ga found the king of Cambay on the limits of Malwa as we noted above.

With the help of the Moslem historians, and in particular Sikandar bin Muhammad, we thus conjecture that Tristão de Ga gave his embassy to Sultan Muzaffar II at Deolah, or at Dhar, each being in Malwa, as both satisfy the criterion of Albuquerque, the father, Barros and Castanheda, *a saber*, that this embassy was given on the confines of both kingdoms.

Albuquerque, Parte III Capitulo LII & Capitulo LIII; Parte IV Capitulo I & Capitulo XII
Barros, Decada II Livro VII Capitulo VII; Livro VIII Capitulo V
Castanheda, Livro III Capitolo XCV, Capitolo CXIIII & Capitolo CXV
Correa, Tomo II Capitulo XXXIX, Capitulo XLI & Capitulo XLIII—Lenda de Afonso de Albuquerque
Goes, Parte III Capitulo XXX & Capitulo XLIIII

BIBLIOGRAPHY

PRINTED SOURCES

PORTUGUESE

1. Albuquerque, Braz de. *Comentários do Grande Afonso de Albuquerque*, Coimbra, Imprensa da Universidade, 1923.
2. Barros, João de. *Da Asia*, Vol. 4, Lisbon, 1777.
3. Castanheda, Fernão Lopes de. *História do Descobrimento & Conquista da India pelos Portugueses*, Coimbra, Imprensa da Universidade, 1928.
4. Correa, Gaspar. *Lendas da India*, Lisbon, 1860.
5. Goes, Damião de. *Crónica do Felicissimo Rei D. Manuel*, Coimbra, Imprensa da Universidade, 1926.

Moslem

1. Firishta. *Tarikh-i-Firishta.* Translated in the *History of the Rise of the Mahomedan Power in India*, London, 1829. English translation by John Briggs.
2. Nizam-ud-din. "Tabaqat-i-Akbari," *Bibliotheca Indica*, Calcutta, 1939.
3. Sikandar bin Muhammad. "Mirat-i-Sikandari," *The Local Muhammadan Dynasties. Gujarat*, London, 1886. English translation by Sir Edward Clive Bayley.

Published Documents

1. *Cartas de Affonso de Albuquerque*, Tomo I, Lisbon, 1884.
   - a) Carta a el-rei de Affonso de Albuquerque—Goa, November 23, 1512: p. 116. Carta XXII
   - b) Carta a el-rei de Affonso de Albuquerque—Cananor, November 30, 1513: p. 135, 136. Carta XXVII
   - c) Carta a el-rei de Affonso de Albuquerque—Cananor, December 3, 1513: p. 193-195. Carta XL
   - d) Carta a el-rei de Affonso de Albuquerque—Cananor, December 4, 1513: p. 202, 239-241. Carta XLI
2. *Cartas de Affonso de Albuquerque*, Tomo II, Lisbon, 1898.
   - a) Instrumento de Affonso de Albuquerque—Goa, March 23, 1514: p. 122. In this document the date of departure of Tristão de Ga and João Gomes from Goa for Cambay is stated: i.e. December 15, 1512.

CHAPTER I   SECTION 10

THE EMBASSY OF DIOGO FERNANDES DE BEJA:
FROM GOA TO SURAT—1514

Not long after Afonso de Albuquerque returned to India from the city of Aden and the Red Sea, he received a message at Cananor from Fernão Martins Evangelho, his factor at Diu, who wrote that a *gelua* had arrived at Diu from the Strait of Meca, in which a messenger came from the *Cadi* of Cairo who carried robes for the king of Cambay, and all his *Guazis*-liegemen, with many blessings, and absolutions, attempting to persuade the king to wage war against the Christians, i.e. against the Portuguese.   The governor of India also learned from the same Fernão Martins Evangelho that Malik Aiyaz, the governor of Diu, had departed Diu for the court of Cambay to dissuade King Muzaffar II from granting the fortress which the Portuguese desired at Diu.   Albuquerque the son records that Malik Aiyaz conveyed gold, silver, jewels, all in plenty, many rich cloths, and two hundred horses to bribe the king and his courtiers upon the *negocio* of Diu, and that Malik Aiyaz, moreover, carried a sword to suborn the king which Albuquerque the father had given to him.

"With the news which Fernão Martins Evangelho wrote concerning the going of Miliqueaz [Malik Aiyaz] to the court of the king of Cambay, the Great Afonso de Albuquerque remained very wroth, and he feared the business of Diu would not have effect, and that he [Malik Aiyaz] would damage it even more than he had done by the letters which he had written [to court upon the subject], of which he had many hopes according to what Milecopi [Malik Gopi] had written to him by Tristão de Ga; and with the intention that it would yet be, he dispatched Diogo Fernandes de Beja and James Teixeira as ambassadors, [*] to discuss this business with the king; and he sent by means of them as presents a collar of embellished gold, and a dagger with [its] scabbard in bluish gold, and a kris of gold, and ten ells of black velvet, and a piece of green brocade from Persia, and two from China, and a chamber pot *de agua ás mãos* and a two-handled flower pot all very well gilded. [**]   And because this embassy was sent with more authority than the others, because of the desire which he had to establish [a] site at Diu, he arranged to provide him [Diogo Fernandes de Beja] with twenty *encaval-*

---

* James Teixeira was accredited to the court of Cambay as second-ambassador and successor to Diogo Fernandes, should the need arise.   (Barros, Decada II Livro X Capitulo I; Castanheda, Livro III Capitolo CXXVII; Correa, Tomo II Capitulo XLIV and Goes, Parte III Capitulo LXIIII)   With James Teixeira the governor sent Francisco Paes as scrivener and Duarte Vaz as interpreter.   (Barros, Decada II Livro X Capitulo I; Castanheda, Livro III Capitolo CXXVII and Goes, Parte III Capitulo LXIIII)

** Braz de Albuquerque has erred.   The chamber pot *de agua ás mãos* and the flower pot were purchased by Diogo Fernandes in Cambay; See the document contained in "Relações com Potentados Africanos e Asiaticos," *Archivo Historico Portuguez*, Vol. II.

gaduras-horsemen, and silver for [the] service of his table, and many peons of the land to be of assistance to his people, and he gave to them a *regimento* of what they were obliged to accomplish." (Albuquerque, Parte IV Capitulo XXI)

The embassy of Diogo Fernandes de Beja, which consisted of twenty Portugals intelligence of Damião de Goes, or twenty-two as Gaspar Correa and Braz de Albuquerque appear to indicate, sailed from Goa in the *Rume* in February of 1514 with each man suitably arrayed. In company with Diogo Fernandes de Beja sailed the *Enxobregas*, which had arrived from Diu, where Fernão Martins Evangelho remained for factor. For these details Castanheda is our surety.

Braz de Albuquerque relates Diogo Fernandes de Beja dispatched Pero Queimado and a Gentile, Ganapatim ("who knew the Guzerate language very well"), to proceed to Cambay to ask for a *seguro*-hostage from the king for the Portuguese embassy, and this after Diogo Fernandes had departed for Cambay, but Castanheda, on the contrary, relates Diogo Fernandes dispatched Pero Queimado upon the matter of the *seguro* before he departed from Goa, and in company with a "Brahman called Anagapatu." (Variously Ganapatim—Albuquerque; Anagapatu, or Ganapatu in another part—Castanheda and Ganda Chatim—Correa)

Diogo Fernandes de Beja and company, continues Castanheda (a sure beacon to light our path), arrived at Chaul after a twenty-seven day voyage from Goa in unpropitious weather. From Chaul Diogo Fernandes dispatched the *Enxobregas* loaded with merchandise for consignment to Fernão Martins Evangelho at Diu. Continuing his voyage, Diogo Fernandes de Beja arrived at the mouth of the River of Çurrate (the Tapti River), where upon the left bank some miles up stream, is situated the city of Surat, a small town at this period, at which Diogo Fernandes de Beja arrived on March 15th 1514.

"And knowing at the bar how Pero Queimado had not yet arrived with the *seguro* from the king, he asked the *regedor*-governor of the city, who was [a] Moor called Destrocão [Dastur Khan], [to send a hostage], and presently he sent one to him, and he [Diogo Fernandes] was received in great style, as the king of Cambay had ordered, because he knew our ambassador was coming. Meâcoje [Miyan Khwaja] and Meâbahu [Miyan Babu], captains of the king, and a brother of Meligupim [Malik Gopi], departed to receive him, accompanied by many people and they brought horses for our people and wagons for their personal effects. Destrocão did not go with them as he was sick with *boubas*-yaws. And the ambassador was received with much love by the Moorish captains [who] brought him to the city, to the house of the governor, by whom they were also well received, and he sent a *cabaya*-Turkish tunic to him, which are clothes of the land, and others to those of his company, which thus they are accustomed to do with foreigners, since dressing one's self in clothes of the land seems to be a great sign of friendship, and which are assurances of peace. The ambassador did not wish to take them, saying he would not take anything, save from the king with whom they would reside. And the governor relating to him that they had been sent by the king of Cambay, and if he did not take them, he would consider it a great dishonor, he took them, and dressed [in them] with those of his company, saying that he did it since they were from the king of Cambay, as they were in his land, and to observe their customs. From that place the ambassador was carried to his lodgings in some houses of Meligupim which were great and rich." (Castanheda, Livro III Capitolo CXXXI)

At a later day Diogo Fernandes de Beja sent a present to the governor by means of Duarte Vaz and Francisco Paes, and thus some other Portuguese, saying to Destrocão (Dastur Khan) that since he, Diogo Fernandes, had honored the governor by taking those *cabayas*, that he would see fit to honor him, and the governor of India, by accepting that present, and to pardon him if, perchance, that present did not please him, since he, Diogo Fernandes de Beja, was a man accustomed to the things of war and did not have the wherewithal to bestow rich presents, and thus Diogo Fernandes dispatched presents to Meâcoje and Meâbahu, to the brother of Meligupim and to his factor, and all received them with good will, and were pleased, although Destrocão refused his at first, but then accepted, and thus apparently to rebuke the Portuguese ambassador.*

After these courtesies Diogo Fernandes commenced to know that Meligupim (Malik Gopi) had fallen into disfavor with the king of Cambay, and that the king had departed in great haste against a fortress which had revolted at a great distance from Surat. Knowing these things the Portuguese ambassador did not wish to proceed to the king of Cambay, until he had certain knowledge of these matters, and excused himself to Destrocão who pressed him to go, stating his *seguro* had not yet arrived from the king. Then:

"Pero Queimado arrived on the 27th of March, and brought with him a letter from the king for the governor [of Surat], in which he told him to give our people whatever was necessary for their journey, as far as the city of Madava [Ahmedabad], where the ambassador was obliged to speak to the king, and another from Meligupim for the governor [of] India in which he declared how wretched he was since he was not in favor with the king so as to be able to serve him as before, as he always desired. And both letters were

---

* Braz de Albuquerque declares one Ruy Paes, and not Francisco Paes, with Duarte Vaz, carried "certain pieces to Desturcão." (Parte IV Capitulo XXI) But Castanheda, who is more explicit, concerning the embassy of Diogo Fernandes de Beja, is also more careful, and Ruy Paes is probably a slip for Francisco Paes. The Destrocão of Castanheda is the Desturcão of Braz de Albuquerque and the Dasturcan of Tome Pires. "Damana [Damão], Çurrate [Surat and] Ranei [Rander] are under the jurisdiction of Dasturcan [a] native Moor of Cambay, [a] nobleman in the land." (Pires, First Book)

43

opened, and the ambassador saw both of them, and knowing by Pero Queimado the disfavor of Meligupim, who had gone to the city of Champanel [Champaner], and the king had gone to succor the castle which had revolted against him, which was at a great distance, he desired to return since he had [a] *regimento* from the governor [enjoining] that by no manner would he winter in Cambay; either he would have concert between the king and himself, or he would not have it." (Castanheda, Livro III Capitolo CXXXI)

Gaspar Correa relates Pero Queimado, in going to the king of Cambay, proceeded from Çurrate (Surat) to Champanel (Champaner). However, Correa indicates Pero Queimado did not meet the king at Champanel; not at Champaner, or at any other place. Braz de Albuquerque and Fernão Lopes de Castanheda must be interpreted as declaring that Pero Queimado met King Muzaffar II at Ahmedabad, and they are better mentors. Perhaps (but not likely) Pero Queimado visited both Champaner and Ahmedabad.

While waiting for his *seguro* at Surat—which Pero Queimado had gone to fetch of the king of Cambay—Castanheda declares Diogo Fernandes de Beja dispatched the *Rume* to explore the coast and to observe the places where Portugal might have a fortress. When the *Rume* returned, Diogo Fernandes desired to depart for Goa in accordance with his *regimento* as Afonso de Albuquerque had instructed him not to settle anything without Malik Gopi. Diogo Fernandes dispatched Duarte Vaz to Desturcão, who, according to Braz de Albuquerque, related to the governor of Surat that the man who came as *seguro* from the king said that the king had departed for the city of Patane (Pattan) against the reys Butos (i.e. against the Rajputs on the northern frontier of Cambay), and that by *regimento* Diogo Fernandes de Beja was obliged by Afonso de Albuquerque to return to Goa before the arrival of the wet monsoon. Castanheda and Braz de Albuquerque relate the governor of Surat contradicted the Portuguese with many strong reasons:

"The Desturcão [Dastur Khan] replied to them by Meababu [Miyan Babu], that since they had already taken their *seguro* [from the king], and all that was necessary for their journey was ready, it did not appear to him to be very good courtesy not to go to the king, nor would he give [a] good account of himself without going to see him, since they came for this [reason]; and that firstly it was necessary to inform the king upon this, and his message arriving, they would be obliged to do as he ordered.

"As Diogo Fernandes de Beja and James Teixeira saw the determination of Desturcão, and that they could not do another thing save what he desired, so as to give [a] good face to their stay, they related to him, that since it appeared he was right, they would do as he ordered, since the captain-general of the Indies would look favorably upon it, [and] that presently they desired to depart for court." (Albuquerque, Parte IV Capitulo XXI)

Albuquerque, Parte IV Capitulo XVI & Capitulo XXI
Barros, Decada II Livro X Capitulo I
Castanheda, Livro III Capitolo CXXVII, Capitolo CXXX & Capitolo CXXXI
Correa, Tomo II Capitulo XLIII & Capitulo XLIV—Lenda de Afonso de
    Albuquerque
Goes, Parte III Capitulo LXIIII
Pires, First Book

BIBLIOGRAPHY

1. Albuquerque, Braz de. *Comentários do Grande Afonso de Albuquerque*, Coimbra, Imprensa da Universidade, 1923.
2. Barros, João de. *Da Asia*, Vol. 4, Lisbon, 1777.
3. Castanheda, Fernão Lopes de. *História do Descobrimento & Conquista da India pelos Portugueses*, Coimbra, Imprensa da Universidade, 1928.
4. Correa, Gaspar. *Lendas da India*, Lisbon, 1860.
5. Goes, Damião de. *Crónica do Felicissimo Rei D. Manuel*, Coimbra, Imprensa da Universidade, 1926.
6. Pires, Tome. *The Suma Oriental*, Vols. I & II, Printed for the Hakluyt Society, London, 1944.

PUBLISHED DOCUMENTS

1. "Relações com Potentados Africanos e Asiaticos," *Archivo Historico Portuguez*, Vol. II, Lisbon, 1904.
    a) Instrumento de Afonso de Albuquerque—Goa, November 8, 1514: p. 454, 455.

CHAPTER I   SECTION 11

THE EMBASSY OF DIOGO FERNANDES DE BEJA: FROM SURAT TO CHAMPANER & FROM CHAMPANER TO AHMEDABAD—1514

Diogo Fernandes de Beja, James Teixeira, Francisco Paes, Duarte Vaz and the Portuguese retinue left Çurrate (Surat) for Madava (Ahmedabad) on March 28th 1514—one day after the arrival of Pero Queimado with the *seguro* the ambassador desired from King Muzaffar II. The governor of Surat, and the factor of Meligupim (Malik Gopi), assigned Diogo Fernandes de Beja thirty-three to thirty-five horses for his party, as they were obliged to proceed on horseback, and twelve wagons for their possessions, and twenty (or thirty) peon archers of Cambay with a mounted guard under one Meâçamadim for their protection.

Being a day or two from Surat, Diogo Fernandes de Beja received a letter from Meligupim, in reply to another that he dispatched from Surat in which Diogo Fernandes asked the Brahman's advice upon whether he should go (or not go) to the king. Meligupim wrote his opinion, *a saber*, he should go. Now exchanging Fernão Lopes de Castanheda for Gaspar Correa, for our source, a movement fraught with danger, we apprehend en route to Ahmedabad:

> "Diogo Fernandes in order to show his grandeur, arriving at some places at which to repose, did not wish to abide over night in houses, but outside in the fields [where] he erected his tent, which was from the Kingdom [i.e. of Portugal], with three props. It was made of canvas which he covered on the outside with white cloths and with *cores entretalhados*-colors in bas-relief, and covered on the inside with cloths of silk from the Strait [of Meca]; and it had a *camara*-chamber and a *sala*-large room and [a] division for the [common] people. In the said tent five hundred people could fit. In the large room there were low chairs, and footstools covered with carpets, and his chamber carpeted, and [with a] gilded bedstead with ornaments and bedspreads of silk and pillows of satin from the Kingdom, of colors. Here his servants and slaves, who were very well dressed, served plate with very rich and magnificent table, where all the men of his company ate many viands and delicacies. . . ."

(Correa, Tomo II Capitulo XLIV)

Passing ahead en route to Ahmedabad, Diogo Fernandes de Beja, to resume the thread of our narrative from Castanheda, received another letter from Meligupim in which the latter requested the ambassador to proceed to Champaner where he was, and to which the Portuguese complied.

DESCRIPTION OF CHAMPANER BY FERNAM LOPES DE CASTANHEDA IN THE *HISTORIA DO DESCOBRIMENTO & CONQUISTA DA INDIA PELOS PORTUGUESES*, LIVRO III CAPITOLO CXXXI

> "It [the city of Champaner] is situated thirty leagues from the sea, in the interior, on a great plain where there is a range, not very round, but very high, so that at the lowest part it is four hundred fathoms high, and it is entirely surrounded by steep rocks. In this range the city is situated,

46

enclosed by walls and towers, and inside the first wall are six others all with very strong walls. The first wall has but one entranceway, through a portal very high and carved by pickax, and it extends beneath the surface for thirty or forty fathoms. In front of this portal lies a very deep fosse, one hundred paces in breadth, over which lies a drawbridge. There are some palaces of the king of Cambay in this city which occupy as much space as Evora, and they are enclosed by walls, served by three iron portals, inside of which only the king and his women repose, and [also] his revenue collectors who go to court, and the officials of his house, and there are magazines of arms and munitions of war, and all the rest consists of gardens which yield fruits as ours, with founts of jasper, and they are all surrounded by many pleasure houses, of which most are of two stories, and the others [of] one floor, and almost all have drains for two sides, and some have walls carved with gold and azure, and others whitened with *betume de gesso*-bitumen of gypsum and clear as egg white, and other confections, with which they remain so white and resplendent as to blind the sight, and the floors are tiled with ornamental tiles. This city has one hundred and thirty thousand hearths." *

Diogo Fernandes de Beja arrived at Champaner on the 4th day of April, at midday, and alighted from his horse in a garden where he divested himself of his travelling apparel for a garb to see Meligupim. As he knew Diogo Fernandes had arrived, Meligupim sent horses to the ambassador and his entourage, and he dispatched many people on horseback and on foot with the ring of many instruments to accompany the ambassador and his people to the houses of Meligupim, where Diogo Fernandes arrived, and from his houses, Meligupim issued forth to greet the ambassador with all the affection at his command. The Brahman Meligupim received a present and a letter from Afonso de Albuquerque, and Diogo Fernandes de Beja resided for three days at Champaner.

After Meligupim had counseled Diogo Fernandes de Beja on the *negocio* of the fortress at Diu which Afonso de Albuquerque so greatly desired, he dispatched the ambassador from Champaner for Ahmedabad where the king resided of the moment. Diogo Fernandes and James Teixeira, and thus others of the Portuguese entourage, received horses from Meligupim and thus wagons and four camels to carry their tents. With the embassy Meligupim dispatched a principal man of his house, and six horse and twenty peons to guide Diogo Fernandes de Beja as far as Ahmedabad.

Approaching Ahmedabad ("which is a greater city than Champaner and more noble in buildings"—Castanheda), Codamacão (Khudawand Khan?), bailiff-major of the sultan of Cambay, received intelligence of the arrival of Diogo Fernandes de Beja. King Muzaffar II had departed Ahmedabad for the

---

* Compare the account of Fernão Lopes de Castanheda with that of João de Barros; See Chapter X of this volume.

recreation of the hunt, and as Codamacão did not know when the king would return, he bade Diogo Fernandes and company to pass the evening in a garden near the city, until Codamacão's message arrived. The next day (*ao outro dia*), during the morning, Codamacão dispatched to Diogo Fernandes a Turk of his house with thirty horse, and a great concourse of men on foot, with many trumpets and ring of instruments to fetch Diogo Fernandes de Beja to the city of Ahmedabad and the apartments of Codamacão.

The entourage of Diogo Fernandes de Beja, Castanheda observes, was amazed by the multitude of the people who inhabited the noble city of Ahmedabad, and thus those of horse, and those who journeyed by foot and thus of the nobility of the buildings, and of the numbers of people who thronged about as they proceeded to their apartments and who, at times, blocked their path seeking to catch a glimpse of the Portuguese. At the residence of Codamacão, Melique Quadragi (Malik Qadir-ji?), son of the governor of Surat, and a page of Sultan Muzaffar II, greeted Diogo Fernandes de Beja at the doorway with all courtesy, and conveyed the ambassador to Codamacão.

> ". . . [the Portuguese] dismounted from their horses, and entered a *sala*-large room where Codamacão awaited them, by whom they were very well received and honored, and Diogo Fernandes presently offered the presents which he carried for him, [*] giving to him a letter from Afonso de Albuquerque. After speaking for awhile, he said to them to rest themselves, and that as soon as the king arrived, who had gone hunting, he would go to the palace and inform him of their arrival, and they would hear from him when he [the king] wished to see them, and he sheltered them in a room of his compartments, where all fitted very spaciously." (Albuquerque, Parte IV Capitulo XXII)

---

* "which were two pieces of satin, one purple, [the] other dark gray: and two others, one of green *camarabãdo* and another of white damask: eighteen ells of *graã*-scarlet-in-grain and a two-handled flower pot of silver, and besides this a goblet which the ambassador added from his house, because in him [i.e. in Codamacão] rested his despatch, good or bad, since he was the closest confidant which the king had at that time. . . ." (Castanheda, Livro III Capitolo CXXXII)

Albuquerque, Parte IV Capitulo XXI & Capitulo XXII
Castanheda, Livro III Capitolo CXXXI & Capitolo CXXXII
Correa, Tomo II Capitulo XLIV—Lenda de Afonso de Albuquerque
Goes, Parte III Capitulo LXIIII

BIBLIOGRAPHY

PRINTED SOURCES

1. Albuquerque, Braz de. *Comentários do Grande Afonso de Albuquerque*, Coimbra, Imprensa da Universidade, 1923.

2. Castanheda, Fernão Lopes de. *História do Descobrimento & Conquista da India pelos Portugueses,* Coimbra, Imprensa da Universidade, 1928.
3. Correa, Gaspar. *Lendas da India,* Lisbon, 1860.
4. Goes, Damião de. *Crónica do Felicissimo Rei D. Manuel,* Coimbra, Imprensa da Universidade, 1926.

PUBLISHED DOCUMENTS

1. "Relações com Potentados Africanos e Asiaticos," *Archivo Historico Portuguez,* Vol. II, Lisbon, 1904.
   a) Instrumento de Afonso de Albuquerque—Goa, November 8, 1514: p. 454, 455.

THE EMBASSY OF DIOGO FERNANDES DE BEJA:
AHMEDABAD—1514

Codamacão dispatched a message to Diogo Fernandes de Beja from the palaces of Sultan Muzaffar II, on the morning of a different day (*ao outro dia*), requesting the ambassador to proceed to the king. To accompany the ambassador, Codamacão charged Melique Quadragi with the task of mustering the ambassador and his retinue. Melique Quadragi proceeded to Diogo Fernandes and carried the ambassador and his people to the palace with great concourse of men on horse, and on foot, and with the interplay of the blare of diverse instruments, and with every Portugal dressed at his finest.* Three Portugals carried the presents of Afonso de Albuquerque. And proceeding in this manner Diogo Fernandes de Beja, on horseback, arrived at the palaces of the sultan of Cambay.

> "The ambassador entered the palaces with Melique Quadragi, and after passing through many courtyards and rooms, they arrived at a very great room [a great veranda upon a beautiful garden states Correa] where at one end, in a *capelinha*-little chapel, facing the door, the king was reclining on a *catle*-divan dressed in a white *cabaya*-Turkish tunic of fine cotton cloth, and on his head, a turban of the same [material**] and many people on foot were placed in order from one end [of the room] to the other, all great lords and captains of people who possessed great revenues; and the ambassador seeing him, made his obeisance after our manner, and with him, all of our people. And presently James Teixeira and he, at his behest, arrived to where he was, and near the *catle*-divan each made his obeisance. And the king received them with great welcome, and stationed both of them near Codamacão and some other lords. Our people went two by two to make their bows to the king as he ordered, and then returned to where they were, and he

---

* "Diogo Fernandes wore a *jornea*-cloak of crimson satin lined with red damask, with many spots of gold and seed pearls for the sleeves; and [a] cap of red velvet, with *chaparia d'ouro*-ornamental, thin, flat strips of gold, and a white feather; and [a] doublet of red satin, well trimmed, lined with blue taffeta, with many edges upon the slashes; *calções*-breeches of blue taffeta with roses of gold; and slippers of velvet upon the feet, with which he did not tread upon carpets [of the audience hall], and went unshod; and at the waist [he wore] a rich sword of gold: James Teixeira thus came in a like manner." (Correa, Tomo II Capitulo XLIV)

** "The king was dressed in white, with a white *touquinha*-headpiece on his head, a dagger of gold at the waist, [and with] a gilded Turkish bow in the hand, with an arrow with which he was amusing himself." (Correa, Tomo II Capitulo XLIV)

showed to all very good face, and showed that he was pleased to see our courtesy.[*]

"This reception having terminated, the ambassador presented the aforementioned gifts [See Albuquerque, Parte IV Capitulo XXI quoted in Chapter I Section 10 of this history] for which the king showed himself well pleased, taking some pieces in his hand, principally the black velvet and looking at them attentively and speaking upon these things with some lords who were with him. Having finished viewing the presents he took a letter of the governor, of which he read presently [as it was written in Arabic—Braz de Albuquerque], which stated how the governor sent his *çalema*-salam, and [how] he was at his service with his entire armada and with all his Portuguese. He received much pleasure from this, and asked about the governor and where he was. This discourse was carried on in this manner. The ambassador spoke to his interpreter [i.e. to Duarte Vaz] and he spoke to another of the king, and he to yet another, who spoke to the king, since this is his custom, and still the custom, and they have it for [a thing of] great state. This conversation having terminated, the king ordered Melique Quadragi to carry the ambassador and our people to the end of the courtyard [and] to give *cabayas*-Turkish tunics to them, those for the ambassador and James Teixeira being of brocade, and velvet for the others, and they dressed themselves, the ambassador declaring he did it for the king's sake, but that this was not his custom. Dressed in *cabayas*,

---

* "The first thing that he [the king of Cambay] asked me was for Your Highness and for the Lady Queen, and how many children you have and of what age was Your Highness. I said to him that you were [a] man of forty-five years and that you have eight children. He was amazed that you have one wife only, and thus he asked me with what Kings Your Highness has war and how far were . . . lands of the sultan [of Egypt] from Portugal. . . ." (Fragmentos, Documentos da India, Cartas Missivas)

I have taken this passage from a letter which has a great tear in it, and a large part of it is missing. Thus the lacunae of the translation belong to the original. The letter is found in an unorganized collection of the Torre do Tombo called the "Fragmentos" and it is neither signed or dated, i.e. where the signature and date usually appear on a Portuguese letter of this period, the letter is missing. The letter, however, is written by Diogo Fernandes de Beja to King Manuel, since I could read it sufficiently during my second visit to Portugal, to make this judgement. Some of the documents of this collection have been identified by the proper employees of the Torre do Tombo, but this letter is unidentified, save for a note which I wrote in Portuguese upon the folder of the letter: "It is written by Diogo Fernandes de Beja ca. 1514." It is difficult to derive much meaning from the document: too much of the letter is missing, although what remains is written in a very clear hand.

51

they returned once more to make reverence to the king after our mode [or to the mode of the land according to Albuquerque, which seems more reasonable, as they were in Moslem garb], and he said to the ambassador that now he would return to his lodgings, and that he should relate to Codamacão everything he wished to say, and that presently he would be dispatched." (Castanheda, Livro III Capitolo CXXXII)

Diogo Fernandes de Beja, James Teixeira and those of their conserve returned to their lodgings.

On another day (*Ao outro dia*), continues Castanheda, Diogo Fernandes related to Codamacão the governor of India had deputed him in embassy to ask for a fortress at Diu, as the king had promised Tristão de Ga. Codamacão declared the sultan had promised a factory, not a fortress, and that for friendship and intercourse with the Kingdom of Cambay, a factory sufficed. Codamacão is either misinformed or privy to an untruth, to judge from the correspondence of Afonso de Albuquerque with King Manuel I, and from the histories of Barros, Castanheda and Damião de Goes. The Moslem sources, unfortunately, are silent as to both the embassies of Tristão de Ga and Diogo Fernandes de Beja to the sultan of Cambay.

Diogo Fernandes propounded the reasons why his countrymen desired a fortress at Diu, urging the security which the Portuguese would derive from it, and that the mere possession of a fortress at Diu was not inimical to friendship between Portugal and Cambay, and that for such a mighty lord as the sultan of Cambay the Portuguese were appealing for a small boon, and with the augmentation of commerce which would follow, His Majesty of Cambay would profit from the fortress, and be enriched. Finally Codamacão declared for the sake of Afonso de Albuquerque he would relate all these reasons to King Muzaffar II. On April 20th 1514, he gave the reply of the king, *a saber*, the Portuguese could have a fortress at Surat, or in an equal manner, a factory anywhere in the kingdom. Castanheda observes Codamacão might have prevailed upon the sultan to grant the Portuguese a fortress at Diu, but he did not choose to confront Malik Aiyaz. Diogo Fernandes replied Afonso de Albuquerque had instructed him only to accept a fortress at Diu, which had a good port, and here the Portugals could *tirar a monte*-lay ships aground if necessary and where their vessels might winter, and that Surat, which the sultan offered, had many inconveniences for the Portuguese. The reply of Diogo Fernandes angered Codamacão. Yet the former prevailed against the Guzerate minister to importune Sultan Muzaffar II *de novo*, and to stress the advantages accruing to His Majesty of Cambay, and that he, Codamacão, should reflect upon the importance of the matter, since the *naos* of the Guzerates would be able to navigate the seas securely, having Cambay peace and concord with the Portuguese, and that the revenues of the sultan would be greater. Counsel the king to grant the Portuguese a fortress at Diu! *Non nobis solum.*

Once again Codamacão returned to the king, and again for the sake of Afonso de Albuquerque.

"Four days later he returned [to Diogo Fernandes], being detained upon this matter for that long, and declared that

52

the king was content to grant a fortress to the governor at
one of four places: Bombaim [Bombay], Çurrate [Surat],
Maim [Kelve Mahim; or possibly Mahim located on Bombay
Island and] Doubez [Dumas?], and [a] factory at Diu or
wherever he wished, [*] and that he would choose one of
these, if he desired peace, because he would not return to
speak with the king [upon this matter], since he would be
greatly angered, and if he did not desire one of those places,
it appeared to him the governor wanted good heart. Still
the ambassador did not wish to accept any of those places,
giving to Codamacão the same reasons why he refused to
accept Surat. And running upon these things, word in word,
Codamacão asked that having peace, would his *naos* (not
carrying spices) be able to navigate securely for Aden or
for the Strait, or would the governor hinder them. The
ambassador replied he did not have reason to send his *naos*
to Aden, or the Strait, having peace and friendship between
the king of Cambay and the king of Portugal, as the king
of Portugal had war with them, and that in true amity per-
force they were friends of friends and enemies of enemies.
From these things the king of Cambay could not escape,
because Tristão de Ga had dealt with them, which Codamacão
denied, although they showed it to him by the *livro* of the
scrivener of Tristão de Ga [i.e. by the book of João Gomes].
He related he did not know the part of the said business,
nor of any other without the king's *chapa*-record, which is
his seal, and furthermore he did not know what profit the
king of Cambay would derive from the friendship of the king
of Portugal if he blocked the navigation of the Strait from
whence he received the greatest gain in his revenues, and
if he would not have this, he did not know what advantage
they could make to him, since to Meliquiaz [Malik Aiyaz],

---

* Braz de Albuquerque declares the sultan was content to offer either Beroche,
Çurrate, Maim, Dumbes or Bacar for the Portuguese fortress. (Parte IV
Capitulo XXII) Beroche, Çurrate and Maim are respectively Broach, Surat
and Kelve Mahim (or Mahim). Visconde de Lagoa conjectures that Dumbes
may have been a port at or near the modern port of Dumas in 21° 06′ lat. N.
and 72° 41′ long. E., on the banks of the Tapti, and that Bacar may be
modern Bhagua in 21° 22′ lat. N. and 72° 38′ long. E.; See *Glossário Toponimico da Antiga Historiografia Portuguesa Ultramarina*, Lisbon, 1950-1954.
Braz de Albuquerque, however, has fallen into error. Bacar is not the name
of a place but a construction called a *casa forte sem bombardas e sem torres*
(i.e. a strong house without bombards or towers) in the letter which we
attribute to Diogo Fernandes de Beja in the collection called Fragmentos. It
also appears from this letter that the Portuguese were offered a fortress at
either Bombay, Kelve Mahim (or Mahim), Damão, Dumas or Surat, or in the
alternative, a *bacar* at Diu.

who was his slave, the governor had given more in the way of privileges. And the ambassador answered, that, although the king of Cambay would not be allowed to navigate for the Strait, he would be able to navigate for Ormuz, Malacca, Pegu, Martaban and Bengal, where he might gather great profits, and more than at Aden and in the Strait, and thus to other parts which have peace with the king of Portugal and are at his service." (Castanheda, Livro III Capitolo CXXXIII)

Perceiving that the Portuguese were not to have a fortress at Diu, and since Diogo Fernandes de Beja had been instructed by Afonso de Albuquerque to accept a fortress only at Diu, and at no other place within the Sultanate of Cambay, he presently desired to leave the country. The ambassador asked Codamacão for an official dispatch to send to the governor of India, which he, Diogo Fernandes, would carry, and taking leave of King Muzaffar II another time at court, he carried *senhas* rich daggers and *senhas* pieces of *camarabandos*-waist bands as presents from the sultan, as did James Teixeira, the second-ambassador, and Codamacão gave a rich *terçado*-broad sword to them and also some pieces of very fine *baetilhas*-fine muslin from Delhi to carry to Afonso de Albuquerque as gifts, and a letter, declaring the king dispatched those things in sign of friendship, and, furthermore, a wild animal called a *ganda* (i.e. a rhinoceros) would be dispatched which Diogo Fernandes would have at Surat.

Albuquerque, Parte IV Capitulo XXII & Capitulo XXIII
Barros, Decada II Livro X Capitulo I
Castanheda, Livro III Capitulo CXXXII & Capitulo CXXXIII
Correa, Tomo II Capitulo XLIV—Lenda de Afonso de Albuquerque
Goes, Parte III Capitulo LXIIII

BIBLIOGRAPHY

PRINTED SOURCES

1. Albuquerque, Braz de. *Comentários do Grande Afonso de Albuquerque*, Coimbra, Imprensa da Universidade, 1923.

2. Barros, João de. *Da Asia*, Vol. 4, Lisbon, 1777.

3. Castanheda, Fernão Lopes de. *História do Descobrimento & Conquista da India pelos Portugueses*, Coimbra, Imprensa da Universidade, 1928.

4. Correa, Gaspar. *Lendas da India*, Lisbon, 1860.

5. Goes, Damião de. *Crónica do Felicissimo Rei D. Manuel*, Coimbra, Imprensa da Universidade, 1926.

PUBLISHED DOCUMENTS

1. *Cartas de Affonso de Albuquerque*, Tomo I, Lisbon, 1884.
   a) Carta a el-rei de Affonso de Albuquerque—Goa, October 25, 1514: p. 333. Carta LXXXI

THE EMBASSY OF DIOGO FERNANDES DE BEJA: FROM AHMEDABAD
TO SURAT, AND THE TERMINATION OF THE EMBASSY—1514

The *negocio* of Diogo Fernandes de Beja (and that of Diu) being concluded, the ambassador of Afonso de Albuquerque departed Ahmedabad on
April 26th 1514, ten days after his arrival at the second capital of the Sultanate
of Cambay, and Diogo Fernandes and his retinue returned with the horses and
wagons which Meligupim (Malik Gopi) assigned to them at the time of their
departure from Champaner. Enroute for Surat, and perhaps via Champaner
(Castanheda and our sources are silent as to the return route), Diogo Fernandes
de Beja encountered a Portugal, one Antonio Afonso, according to Castanheda,
who the governor dispatched to him with letters and with money. As Albuquerque had forbidden the ambassador to winter in Cambay, Antonio Afonso
apparently came as a messenger of the governor's concern for Diogo Fernandes
and retinue, but I have not ascertained why the governor was so anxious that
Diogo Fernandes de Beja should not winter in Cambay.

Diogo Fernandes de Beja and his people arrived at Surat on May 8th 1514
after the force of the southwest monsoon had set in on that coast, and Diogo
Fernandes was obliged to consume his time and *fazenda* at Surat for the duration of the rainy season.

> "Ten days after his arrival, the *ganda* [rhinoceros] arrived.
> It is a wild animal of roughly the bulk of a large barrel and
> [with] short forelegs and after appendages, and entirely
> covered by *côchas* [lit. shells, but in the sense of plates
> here], save at the belly, and the head as a pig's, and in the
> middle of the forehead, a very sharp horn, a palm or more in
> length. These animals breed in the wilderness of the Indian
> interior, and the Indians call them *gandas*, and I believe they
> are the rhinoceros, [an animal] which Diodoro [Diodorus
> Siculus, *Library of History*, Book III, 35] says fights with
> the elephant and kills it. A captain of the king of Cambay
> brought this [animal], well accompanied by people, and thus
> he delivered it to the ambassador with great fete of music.
> And the ambassador gave to him a piece of white satin and
> ten pardaos in money." (Castanheda, Livro III Capitolo
> CXXXIII)

Afonso de Albuquerque dispatched the *ganda* to King Manuel I. He
arrived safely in Portugal, but when the king of Portugal sent it to the Pope
as a gift the *ganda* was lost at sea (See Chapter XV). The rhinoceros was an
animal virtually unknown to 16th century Europe; along with the larger African
and Asian quadrupeds, however, the rhinoceros was well known at ancient
Rome, even as early as the time of Pompey the Great, who, according to Pliny
the Elder (*Natural History*, Book VIII, XXVIII, XXIX), displayed a rhinoceros
to the Romans at his games 55 B.C. The Emperor Commodus (180-192) by
his own hand destroyed rhinoceros, two elephants, five hippopotami and a
camelopard during the course of two successive days: Cassius Dio *Roman
History*, Epitome of Book LXXIII. And Aelian (*Nature of Animals*, Book

XVII, 44) declares the description of the appearance and shape of the rhinoceros would be stale three times over as many Romans and Greeks were familiar with the animal, so commonplace had the rhinoceros become to the Romans of the third century of our era.

> "In July the ambassador wintering at Surat sent Pero Queimado to Madaual [Ahmedabad] with letters to Codamacāo concerning seven Christian slaves who fled enroute coming to Surat, who he knew were at his house. And Codamacāo, reading the letters, did not wish to give the slaves, and he said to Pero Queimado if he could find them, he could have them, and neither he nor Melique Quadragi, to whom he [Diogo Fernandes] wrote upon the instance, responded to the ambassador. And the ambassador seeing he did not have remedy for those slaves, searched for his embarkation." (Castanheda, Livro III Capitolo CXXXIII)

Diogo Fernandes de Beja secured from the factors of Meligupim, after many delays and inconveniences, "three *zambucos*, which they call *cotumbas*, at the cost of Meligupim"—Castanheda. (Albuquerque says Desturcāo sent the three *cotumbas* "which are some small ships".) With these Diogo Fernandes de Beja, and retinue, and *ganda*, departed from Surat on September 13th 1514 and returned to Goa.

Albuquerque, Parte IV Capitulo XXIII
Barros, Decada II Livro X Capitulo I
Castanheda, Livro III Capitolo CXXXIII
Correa, Tomo II Capitulo XLIV—Lenda de Afonso de Albuquerque
Goes, Parte III Capitulo LXIIII

BIBLIOGRAPHY

PRINTED SOURCES

1. Albuquerque, Braz de. *Comentários do Grande Afonso de Albuquerque*, Coimbra, Imprensa da Universidade, 1923.
2. Barros, João de. *Da Asia*, Vol. 4, Lisbon, 1777.
3. Castanheda, Fernão Lopes de. *História do Descobrimento & Conquista da India pelos Portugueses*, Coimbra, Imprensa da Universidade, 1928.
4. Correa, Gaspar. *Lendas da India*, Lisbon, 1860.
5. Goes, Damião de. *Crónica do Felicissimo Rei D. Manuel*, Coimbra, Imprensa da Universidade, 1926.

CHAPTER I   SECTION 14

THE VOYAGE OF LOPO FERNANDES TO DIU—1514

In this year of 1514 Lopo Fernandes, we are informed by the governor of India, sailed to Diu in the *Enxobregas* with merchandise of the king (i.e. in company with Diogo Fernandes de Beja who sailed from Goa in February and departed company with the *Enxobregas* at Chaul, as we stated in Section 10 of this Chapter). From our source we learn Lopo Fernandes returned to Portuguese India in the same year.

BIBLIOGRAPHY

PUBLISHED DOCUMENTS

1. *Cartas de Affonso de Albuquerque*, Tomo I, Lisbon, 1884.
   a) Carta de Affonso de Albuquerque para el-rey—Goa, October 25, 1514: p. 323.   Carta LXXV
   b) Carta de Affonso de Albuquerque para el-rey—Cochin, December 15, 1514: p. 364.   Carta XCVIII

CHAPTER I   SECTION 15

THE VOYAGE OF LUIS DANTAS AND CHRISTOVAM DE BRITO TO DIU—1514

Luis Dantas sailed from Portugal with the *São Miguel* in this same year of 1514 in a fleet of four (or five) vessels: captain Christovão de Brito. Francisco Pereira (in his ship) arrived upon the bar of Goa and then Luis Dantas ca. August-September 1514.   The *São Miguel* carried six hundred quintals of copper and another eighty quintals of ivory.   Afonso de Albuquerque, the governor of India, dispatched Luis Dantas in the *São Miguel* with great haste, as he writes the king in a letter dated Goa October 20th 1514, to sell the copper and ivory and to fetch a supply of *alaqueqas*-cornelians and indigo, and this by the instrumentality of Jorge Rodrigues the factor of the ship.

EXTRACT OF A LETTER OF AFONSO DE ALBUQUERQUE TO THE KING D. MANUEL

Dated Cochin, 10th December 1514

"Lord—By other letters I have written to Your Highness how Luis Dantas and the *nao São Miguel* arrived at India before Christovão de Brito and how I presently dispatched the *nao* and six hundred quintals of copper which came in it, and eighty of ivory, which he brought from Mozambique, to Diu, as soon as he arrived upon the bar of Goa; Christovão de Brito came after this, and to give dispatch to his *fazenda*, and to fetch the *nao* [of Luis Dantas], I granted him a *caravela* in which he sailed to Diu to search for the *nao*, in which he carried all of his merchandise, and that of his brother, and I gave to him a written order (*mandado*) for Luis Dantas to deliver the *nao* to him as Your Highness ordered and commanded.   Christovão de Brito departed from Diu, and his pilot watched so carefully the land near Chaul,

57

that he ran upon a *baixa*-shoal, coming with the *prumo*-plumb in the hand, as at night it appeared to be five fathoms.[*] The *nao* was lost but he saved the money which he carried from Diu. He did not bring any *alaqeqas*-cornelians nor indigo, nor clothing for Sofala. . . ." (*Cartas de Affonso de Albuquerque*, Tomo I, Carta XCV 1514-Dezembro 10 Letter of Afonso de Albuquerque to the King—Cochin)

Afonso de Albuquerque in yet another letter to King Manuel I, dated Cochin December 18th 1514, informs the king that Luis Dantas, arriving at the port of Diu, discharged the governor's *regimento* to the letter, and that Miliquiaz (Malik Aiyaz) had written the governor praising the good order with which Luis Dantas concerted his business at the port. However coming to Goa, Luis Dantas suffered the same fate as Christovão de Brito, as Albuquerque notes in this letter, only partially preserved, and lost the *caravela* in front of Chaul saving a great part of the merchandise and artillery. The commercial voyages of Luis Dantas and Christovão de Brito terminated then in these unhappy circumstances.

---

* "When I went from Diu for Chaul, a pilot of Portugal came in the *nao* [i.e. the *São Miguel*], and he ran it upon a *penedo*-rock, which they say was unknown. Lord I had rather died a thousand deaths than have that disaster happen to me, because lord, I will never be able to smile again, and if I had not been so weak, I should have gone quite mad." (*Cartas de Affonso de Albuquerque*, Tomo III, 1514-Novembro 29 Letter of Christovão de Brito to the King—Chaul)

BIBLIOGRAPHY

PUBLISHED DOCUMENTS

1. *Cartas de Affonso de Albuquerque*, Tomo I, Lisbon, 1884.
   a) Carta a el-rei de Affonso de Albuquerque—Goa, October 20, 1514: p. 265, 266. Carta LI
   b) Carta a el-rei de Affonso de Albuquerque—Cochin, December 10, 1514: p. 356, 357. Carta XCV
   c) Carta a el-rei de Affonso de Albuquerque—Cochin, December 18, 1514: p. 365, 366. Carta XCIX
2. *Cartas de Affonso de Albuquerque*, Tomo III, Lisbon, 1903.
   a) Carta de Christovão de Brito para el-rei D. Manuel—Chaul, November 29, 1514: p. 100.
3. *Cartas de Affonso de Albuquerque*, Tomo IV, Lisbon, 1910.
   a) Carta de Affonso de Albuquerque a el-rei D. Manuel—Goa, September 26, 1514: p. 189.

CHAPTER I SECTION 16
JOAM PAES AND OTHER PORTUGALS AT DIU—1516

In a letter dated January 3rd 1517, Dom Guterre de Monroy, the captain of Goa, informs Lopo Soares de Albergaria, the governor of India (1515-1518), that many Portuguese were at Diu and that amongst them was one João Paes with merchandise of the king.

BIBLIOGRAPHY
DOCUMENTS

1. Letter of Dom Guterre de Monroy to Lopo Soares—January 3, 1517. Corpo Cronológico: Parte I Maço 21 Documento 2. Cf. Fundo Antigo, Número 804, also of the Torre do Tombo, where some of the commercial particulars of the voyage are noted.

CHAPTER I SECTION 17
FERNAM MARTINS EVANGELHO DISCOVERED *DE NOVO* AT DIU—1517

In 1517 Fernão de Alcaçova came to Portuguese India with the office of Overseer of the King's Revenues (*vedor da fazenda*), not accountable to Lopo Soares de Albergaria, the governor of India (1515-1518), or anyone else, save the king, and promptly dispatched Fernão Martins Evangelho to Diu from Goa as factor. Fernão Martins Evangelho sold large quantities of copper, ivory and alum, the property of the king, and purchased a great quantity of commodities. Fernão Martins Evangelho, the reader will recall, passed to Diu in 1513 in the fleet of Afonso de Albuquerque where he remained as factor until 1515 (?).

BIBLIOGRAPHY
PUBLISHED DOCUMENTS

1. "Cartas de Quitação del Rei D. Manuel," *Arquivo Historico Português*, Vol. X, Lisbon, 1916.
   a) Carta no. 778, Pero Guomez da Rosa a fez em Lixboa, a 7 de Novembro de 1543: p. 12, 13.

✠ ✠ ✠

EXTRACT OF THE ROYAL COMMAND (*REGIMENTO*) WHICH FERNAM DE ALCASOVA, OVERSEER OF THE KING'S REVENUES (*VEADOR DA FAZENDA*), CARRIED TO INDIA IN THE YEAR 1517

"We have forbidden that our factors of our factories, and scriveners of the same, shall trade in any commodities, or [likewise] some [persons] by reason of the liberty that we have granted to those who are now serving us, because we have it for [a] thing very prejudicial to our service, and now we consider it for [a] good thing likewise not to [permit] trade in *mamtimentos*-provisions in one thing and another, under penalty that they will be removed from their offices, and lose all their wages; and even as you arrive we order you to arrange to proclaim it at Cochin, and afterwards in all the other factories, and of the *provicação*-provision you shall make [a] public ceremony so no one may allege ignorance, and you shall place in execution the said penalties to those who violate it. And you shall place in the offices our servants, persons that serve us well and loyally, until you shall have informed us, and to provide for whomever shall serve us in them. And we order you not to permit any of our factors of India to carry burlap, thus of merchandise which comes from here, as well as those of that place of India, nor any *caixas* [a type of Indian coin]; and all you will take possession of for us, and prescribe it against them, and sell it and usefully employ the rest as will be of profit to us; and we command that you shall take great and special care that thus you do it.

"We have information that the captains of the fortresses purchase *mamtimentos*-provisions inside of the places at which they are located, from the hands of the merchants and persons who bring them there to sell; it results in a great disservice to us, for which we prohibit and order that they will not be able to do it; they will only be able to arrange to buy them outside of the said places at which they are Captains, in the places where they find them, and from thence to arrange for their sale, and in this they are to employ themselves to best account. And if they do the contrary, they will lose all their wages which they will have from us, and they will not have them again, save by our special order, and furthermore all [the] provisions which thus they purchase."

Archivo Portuguez Oriental, Fasciculo 5.º 1.ª Parte, Nova Goa, 1865.

In the said volume there are numerous documents which refer to Fernão de Alcaçova, and they are amongst the oldest documents that have been preserved in India of the primeval period of the Portuguese conquests. These documents, and many others, principally pertaining to a later period, were published by J. H. da Cunha Rivara.

Fernão de Alcaçova sailed to India from Portugal in the outward bound fleet, captain Antonio de Saldanha, and having disputes with Lopo Soares de Albergaria, principally concerning their respective commands, and powers, Fernão de Alcaçova returned to Portugal in the homeward bound fleet, having tasted India for a few months only, and to no result.

SUNDRY VOYAGES TO DIU—1518-1521, AND THE EMBASSY OF
RUI FERNANDES (OR PERO SOARES)—1521

With the re-establishment of the Portuguese factory at Diu, under the
superintendence of Fernão Martins Evangelho, in 1517, the tempo of Portuguese intercourse with the Kingdom of Cambay accelerates. Voyages to the
port of Diu become commonplace and in the year 1518 we find (in Castanheda,
Livro IV Capitolo XXXII) João Gonçalves de Castelo Branco, in a *caravela*,
and Manuel de Lacerda and Garcia da Costa, in their *naos*, at the port of Diu,
and from the same reliable source we discern many Portuguese vessels trading
at Diu at this time.

Diogo Lopes de Sequeira (1518-1521), the governor of India, dispatched
Christovão de Sa with three galleys to wage war on the coast of Cambay in
1519: captains, besides himself, Dom Jorge de Menezes and Jorge Barreto de
Beja. The *fustas* of Malik Aiyaz were attacking the ships of the Portuguese
and those of their allies. Diogo Lopes, therefore, ordered Christovão de Sa
to pardon nothing upon the Cambay coast, and Castanheda (Livro V Capitolo
XIIII) asserts he executed the orders of the governor and returned to Goa.
Castanheda (and thus Barros, who notices the voyage in Decada III Livro III
Capitolo VIII) are silent as to the particulars of the activities of Christovão de
Sa on the coast of Cambay. We are also informed by Castanheda and Barros
that Antonio de Saldanha, the years of 1518 and 1519, was active off the coast
of Diu, plundering the *naos* of the Moslems with a fleet.

These are not interesting matters (to my taste), nor unusual, but rather
commonplace in the time of the governorship of Diogo Lopes de Sequeira, since
the Portuguese had now visited every corner of the western coast of India, and
a good portion of the eastern littoral as well.

Diogo Lopes de Sequeira visited Diu in 1520, returning from a voyage to
the Red Sea and Ormuz with a large fleet, and twice in 1521, with great fleets,
desiring the fortress of Diu which King Manuel, his lord, now directed him to
have, either in peace or with war, and on each occasion the governor of India
was deterred from forcing a violent conclusion to this matter of the fortress by
the formidable defenses of the city.

In February of 1521 Diogo Lopes de Sequeira, arriving before Diu with
a large fleet, delivered Rui Fernandes to Fernão Martins Evangelho, the Portuguese factor, to provide with the wherewithal for a journey to humbly solicit,
once again, a fortress at Diu, and once again at the foot of the Cambay throne.*

---

* Gaspar Correa (Tomo II Capitulo XV), however, declares Pero Soares was
the ambassador accredited to the court of Cambay at this time, or rather not
quite at this time, since Correa opines (and apparently wrongly, after his usual
wont) that Diogo Fernandes de Beja, who Diogo Lopes left upon Diu with a
fleet when the governor departed for Ormuz, as we will see, dispatched Pero
Soares to the king of Cambay. Castanheda, strangely, has not noticed an
embassy to Sultan Muzaffar II at this time, and the credible particulars are
gathered from Barros, Decada III Livro IV Capitulo IX and Livro VI Capitulo
VI.

Diogo Lopes also dispatched Antonio Correa, João de Coimbra and Diogo de la Puente to the rio de Madrefaba (Jafarabad), five leagues east of Diu, and in a *cotia* to reconnoiter the river and its banks, and to observe if said were a suitable place to erect a fortress. João de Coimbra and Diogo de la Puente, the former being the *piloto mór da India*, and the latter expert in the art of masonry and construction (*mestre das obras de pedraria*), departed in a small bark from the *cotia*, and ascended the river to the town of Madrefaba to gather intelligence of the land, and they were imprisoned by the Moors of the village and forwarded to Melique Saca (Malik Ishak), the son of Malik Aiyaz, who governed Diu in the absence of his father, who amongst other occupations, including a war against the Rajputs, had proceeded to court once again, and once again to dissuade King Muzaffar II from granting the Portuguese a fortress at Diu. Melique Saca delivered João de Coimbra and Diogo de la Puente to Diogo Lopes de Sequeira as if to emphasize, we might say, the state of semi-warfare which had persisted between the crowns of Portugal and Cambay from the time of Dom Francisco de Almeida (1505-1509)—each contestant sparring with his opposite—yet fearing to come to decisive blows—so that the Guzerates had not secured the peace on the seas which they desired for the secure and easy navigation of their *naos*, nor had the Portuguese obtained the fortress at Diu which they desired, and greatly desired, for the security of their nationals and *fazenda* at the prosperous port of Diu. João de Coimbra and Diogo de la Puente were delivered to the governor before Antonio Correa in the *cotia* returned from the mouth of the Madrefaba, where he had been bombarded by the Moors of the land. The governor was informed by his mission that the town of Madrefaba was a suitable site to erect a good fortress. The governor decided to winter at Ormuz, following which, he purposed to return to Madrefaba and erect a fortress at that location, not having another at Diu.

The embassy of Rui Fernandes (or Pero Soares), to which we referred above, was as fruitless as the embassy of Tristão de Ga in 1512-1513 and that of Diogo Fernandes de Beja in 1514 upon the *negocio* of the fortress at Diu. Rui Fernandes, we are informed in a brief notice by Barros, when he arrived at Champanel (Champaner), where the king was, comprehended that Malik Aiyaz had already settled with the king of Cambay the reply that was granted to him, *a saber*, that the Portuguese could not have a fortress at Diu, and from Barros we learn that Rui Fernandes was unable to prevail against those lords at court, who were hostile to Malik Aiyaz and his affairs, to intervene with the king against Malik Aiyaz on behalf of Rui Fernandes. Rather the king replied to Diogo Fernandes de Beja, who the governor left upon Diu with a fleet of three ships to await the reply to the message that he dispatched with Rui Fernandes, to this end, that Malik Aiyaz desired the Portuguese to have a fortress at Diu, but that with some occupations which he, the king, had, he had not dispatched Rui Fernandes, but that as the occasion would offer, he would dispatch the ambassa-dor with message for the governor of India.* With this reply Diogo Fernandes de Beja sent to gather the property of his king, little by little, so as to avoid

---

* Correa relates the king placed the ambassador on the "mountain of Champanel, where he died" and thus apparently as a prisoner of King Muzaffar II of Cambay; See Correa, Tomo II Capitulo XXI.

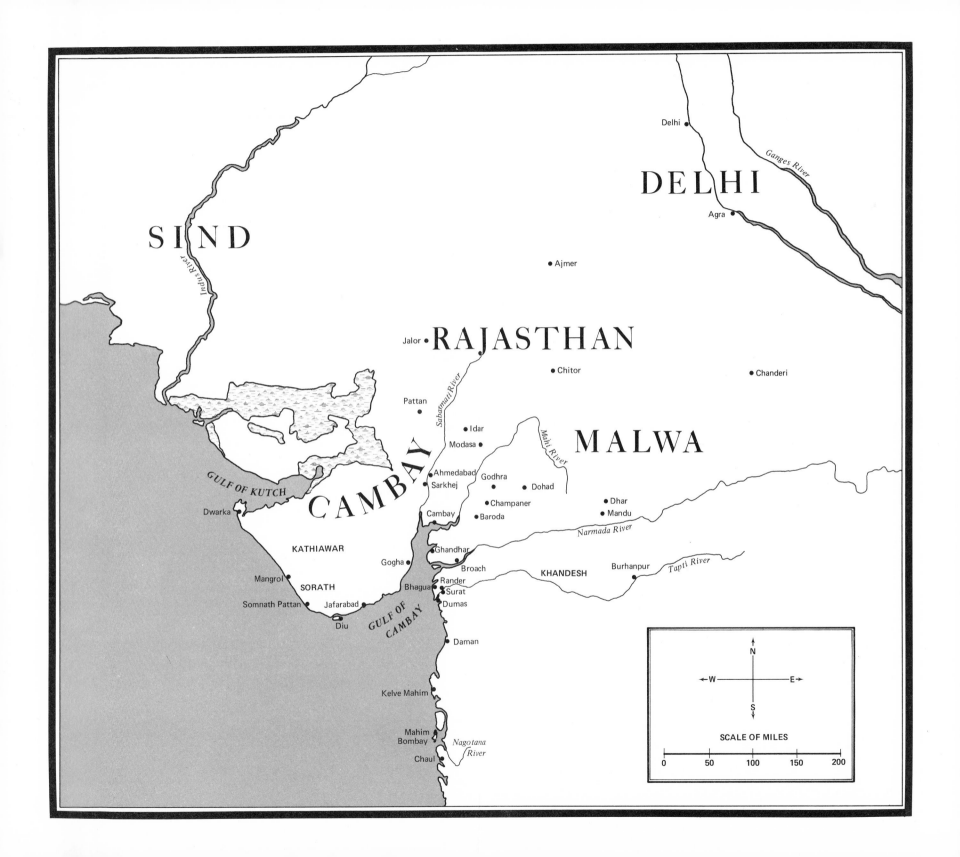

Delhi

Ganges River

DELHI

Agra

Indus River

SIND

Ajmer

Jalor

RAJASTHAN

Chitor

Chanderi

Pattan

Sabarmati River

Idar

Modasa

Mahi River

MALWA

Ahmedabad

Godhra

Sarkhej

Dohad

Dhar

GULF OF KUTCH

CAMBAY

Champaner

Mandu

Dwarka

Cambay

Baroda

Narmada River

KATHIAWAR

Ghandhar

Gogha

Broach

KHANDESH

Burhanpur

Tapti River

Mangrol

SORATH

Bhagua

Rander

Somnath Pattan

Jafarabad

Surat

Dumas

Diu

GULF OF CAMBAY

Daman

Kelve Mahim

Mahim

Bombay

Nagotana River

Chaul

SCALE OF MILES

0   50   100   150   200

suspicion, and then Fernão Martins Evangelho with his assistants from the factory of Diu, and then Diogo Fernandes de Beja issued a declaration of war against the Kingdom of Cambay, but instead of scourging his adversaries of Cambay, was scourged instead by the mobile *fustas* of Diu and obliged to fly to Diogo Lopes de Sequeira at Ormuz.

From Ormuz Diogo Lopes de Sequeira (1518-1521), the governor of India dispatched Diogo Fernandes de Beja in the *São Matheus* in August of 1521, with three ships: captains Nuno Fernandes de Macedo, Manuel de Macedo and Gaspar Doutel. They departed on August 20th to proceed to Diu to wage implacable war against the Moslem Kingdom of Cambay, for into such a sad state had the relations between Portugal and Cambay degenerated at the term of the reign of King Manuel I and the First Age of the Portuguese intercourse with that part of India. Diogo Fernandes fared no better with a second try at the *fustas* of Diu, which sank the ship of Gaspar Doutel, and captured twenty-five Portuguese, and nearly sank the ship of Diogo Fernandes de Beja and gave great work to Nuno Fernandes de Macedo. Finally with a storm which intervened the *fustas* departed for Diu and Diogo Fernandes proceeded to Chaul.

Diogo Lopes de Sequeira was not less unfortunate in coming again for Diu shortly after the return of Diogo Fernandes de Beja. Enroute he captured a Moorish vessel and distributed the captives among the *naos* of his fleet. And being off Diu the Moorish prisoners of the *Santa Maria da Serra*, captain Aires Correa, as desperate men, had manner by which they started a fire, which as it spread, ignited the gunpowder in the powder-magazine, and in the phrase of João de Barros, tossed the decks in the air and placed the hull on the bottom.*
Aires Correa perished in this disaster, and with him the greater part of the company of his ship, and Diogo Lopes de Sequeira, since he brought in the *Santa Maria* all the munitions and supplies with which he hoped to erect a fortress at Madrefaba, and Dom Aleixo de Menezes (who governed India in the absence of the governor) had not rendezvoused at the place where Diogo Lopes had expected him with his people and stores for the fortress, and also, as he knew from Diogo Fernandes, that Malik Aiyaz had prepared to receive him wherever he might land, either at Diu or at Madrefaba, Diogo Lopes de Sequeira, the governor of India, gave over the attempt to erect a fortress at either, and proceeded to Chaul to erect a fortress in this city of the Deccan, and to which business Diogo Lopes had dispatched Fernão Camelo when he departed for Ormuz earlier in this year of 1521, the last of the reign of King Manuel I of Portugal, and the last for our discussion of the First Age of Portuguese relations with the ancient and Moslem Kingdom of Cambay.

---

* Castanheda (Livro V Capitolo LXXIII) indicates the captives were taken, not from a Moorish vessel captured enroute as Barros states (Decada III Livro VI Capitulo VII), but were taken aboard at Ormuz at the departure of the governor, which, according to Castanheda, occurred at the end of September 1521. Upon the matter of the captives Correa (Tomo II Capitulo XVIII) chimes with Barros, *a saber*, the captives were taken enroute.

Barros, Decada III Livro I Capitulo X; Livro III Capitulo I & Capitulo VIII; Livro IV Capitulo VII, Capitulo VIII & Capitulo IX; Livro VI Capitulo VI & Capitulo VII

Castanheda, Livro IV Capitolo XXXII; Livro V Capitolo XIIII, Capitolo XLV, Capitolo XLVI, Capitolo XLVII, Capitolo XLVIII, Capitolo XLIX, Capitolo L, Capitolo LI, Capitolo LIII, Capitolo LXVII, Capitolo LXVIII & Capitolo LXXII

Correa, Tomo II Capitulo XI, Capitulo XIII, Capitulo XV, Capitulo XVIII & Capitulo XXI—Lenda de Diogo Lopes de Sequeira

Goes, Parte IV Capitulo XXVIII, Capitulo XXXVI, Capitulo XLV, Capitulo LX & Capitulo LXIX

BIBLIOGRAPHY

PRINTED SOURCES

1. Barros, João de. *Da Asia*, Vols. 5 & 6, Lisbon, 1777.
2. Castanheda, Fernão Lopes de. *História do Descobrimento & Conquista da India pelos Portugueses*, Coimbra, Imprensa da Universidade, 1928 & 1929.
3. Correa, Gaspar. *Lendas da India*, Lisbon, 1860.
4. Goes, Damião de. *Crónica do Felicissimo Rei D. Manuel*, Coimbra, Imprensa da Universidade, 1926.

DOCUMENTS

1. Letter of Jeronimo de Sousa to the King D. Manuel—Cochin, November 5, 1518. Gavetas: Gaveta 20 Maço 1 Documento 24.

REFERENCES TO THE PORTUGUESE UPON THE COASTS OF BALUCHISTAN AND SIND

In two sixteenth century rutters (*livros de marinharia*), the so-called *livros de marinharia* of João de Lisboa and Bernardo Fernandes, the rutter of the Portuguese voyage from Ormuz to Diu is given. We learn the Portuguese were accustomed to sail the coasts of Baluchistan (*costa dos Noutaques*), Sind and Cambay at certain times of the year. Both rutters declare that Pero Lopes— who was a pilot in the armada of Afonso de Albuquerque, which proceeded to the Red Sea in 1513—discovered a river in twenty-four degrees of the north. This is the mighty Indus, entering the Arabian Sea in that part of India (or rather modern Pakistan) called Sind, which in the period under consideration was an independent kingdom of the Moslems. The Portugals had frequent occasion to pass from Ormuz, where they possessed a fortress, to the parts of India in the time of King Manuel I (1495-1521), and they were undoubtedly frequent visitors and viewers of the coasts of Baluchistan and the Kingdom of Sind. Notwithstanding, the Portuguese sources are oblivious to virtually all that concerns the Portuguese connection with these regions of western India. From the Portuguese captains and mariners, as well as from his native informants, Tome Pires understood:

> "These Naitaques [people of Baluchistan] are Gentiles, without Moors amongst them. They are numerous. It is [a] large land. It extends into the interior. They do not have

[a] king. They live in tribes. None of these has ever received the name of Muhammad. They have their own language. They do not have cities. They have villages in the *serras nomtes*. This river [what river? the Dasht] makes them very strong because it floods the flat land. The land has many provisions: wheat, barley [and] fruits. The greater part of these people are pirates. They sail in light barks. They are archers. As many as two hundred [archers] go to sea and rob as the occasion offers, and sometimes they proceed as far as Ormuz. They enter the narrows to make assaults and this is their manner. They carry bows, swords [and] lances, and they are not very civilized men. On account of the weather they often anchor at the mouth of this river, and it is [a] bay with shallows and rock. Sometimes the Naitaques seize any ship which comes there, and other times they go to the Kingdom of Cambay, to its ports, and if they find [anything] they steal [it] in whatever place they can. They fear no one. They do not have river-retreats in their lands. They are numerous in these parts. They are known as men of this manner.

"Those who sow and plough in land have many horses and mares in which they are like Bedouins, likewise, stealing as the occasion offers. They have peace and friendship with the Resputes [Rajputs], and they pardon nothing of the Moors, and they wish [to pardon] other people. The Naitaques have a close affinity to the Resputes, and living amongst [the] Moors, their lands surrounded for so long, they have never been able to subjugate them. They are valiant highwaymen."

BENGAL

CHAPTER II   SECTION 1

PRIMEVAL PORTUGUESE NOTICES OF THE KINGDOM OF BENGAL

The Lusitanians of King Manuel I (1495-1521) acquired a very smart knowledge of the coast line of western India. With reference to the coasts of Cambay, the indomitable Portugals navigated the sea-littoral from Bombay in the south, to Kelve Mahim and Surat in the north, and beyond, and from the delta of the Indus River—on whose waters Alexander the Great sailed to the shores of the Indian Ocean—to the wealthy and well-fortified city of Diu governed by the astute Malik Aiyaz. The bows of the Portuguese breasted the waters of the Gulf of Cambay to a greater extent than our sources will admit, and the Portuguese journeyed to the noble cities of Champaner and Ahmedabad, in the interior of the Sultanate of Cambay, and to others, as we noted when we discussed the embassies of Gonçalo Homem and Antonio do Loureiro (1511-1512), Tristão de Ga (1512-1513) and Diogo Fernandes de Beja (1514). But regarding the coast of eastern India, the Portuguese possessed a less certain apprehension of the particulars of its extent and configuration. The Portuguese knew of the Kingdom of Bengal, lying at the head of the bay of the same name, by means of intelligence which they procured from the Asian merchants who traded there. This state of affairs endured until the time of the governorship of Lopo Soares de Albergaria (1515-1518). In his time the Portugals drank the waters of the sacred Ganges where the soldiers of Alexander feared to tread.

In the *Lendas da India* Gaspar Correa records Dom Francisco, the viceroy of India (1505-1509), dispatched four men, and presumably Portugals (we are not advised as to their names), to the Coromandel coast in *naos* of the merchants of Cochin.

> "The viceroy gave to the said persons many *assinados de seguros*-signed passes which they were obliged to give to merchants who desired to come to Cochin with their *drogas*-spices, and with any other merchandise, and he counselled them that if they were able, they should pass to Pegu, and to Bengal, and to observe all, and that they should take all the information which time and circumstance offered. And above all he counselled them to take great information of the house of St. Thomas the Apostle which was there [i.e. in Coromandel], since he had information [of this] from some men of Malabar, who related they were Christians of the doctrine of the Blessed Apostle, of which he greatly desired to know the truth. The Viceroy gave to these men some merchandise so that they would appear to be merchants. Two of these men died, and the other two returned, and gave to the Viceroy great intelligence of all those things, for which the Viceroy dispatched them to the King with their *carta de crença*-credentials to inform the King of what they knew and saw. . . ."   (Correa, Tomo I Capitulo X)

The intelligence of Correa suggests a Portuguese voyage to Bengal as early as 1507/1508. However we are not explicitly informed the Portuguese visited either Bengal or Pegu, and João de Barros and Antonio Galvão must be interpreted as denying a Portuguese visit to either land at this time, and Barros and Galvão are engines of sufficient force to demolish any conjecture erected upon the intelligence of Gaspar Correa: to wit that any Portugal, or group of Portugals, visited the Moslem Kingdom of Bengal before the time of the governorship of Lopo Soares de Albergaria (1515-1518).

The Portuguese however desired the wealth of Bengal, and sought to create a favorable impression amongst the merchants of the kingdom, as we see in a notice of Ruy de Brito, the captain of Malacca from 1511 to 1514.

EXTRACT OF THE LETTER OF RUY DE BRITO TO AFONSO DE ALBUQUERQUE

Dated Malacca, 6th January 1514

"Item—Later [i.e. in the year 1513] a junk belonging to the Bendara [of Malacca], and the merchants of the land, departed from here for Bengal. There it proceeded to winter and to fetch clothing and merchandise. I requested the Bendara to dispatch that junk to those parts so as to give true information about us to the land, and thus, so they would come here without fear, and that he would write to them in detail of our truth and justice, and of the manner we treat the merchants, since our enemies do not give true information of our things." (*Cartas de Affonso de Albuquerque*, Tomo III, 1514—Janeiro 6 Letter of Ruy de Brito to Afonso de Albuquerque—Malacca)

Afonso de Albuquerque in a letter directed to the king, dated Cananor November 30th 1513 also renders notice of Portuguese contacts with Bengal, and with many other lands at this time. The governor of India relates the factors of Cochin had dispatched *naos* with merchandise to Bengal, Pegu, Tenasserim, Sumatra, Malacca and Siam (*Sarnao*) towards the east, and as far as Zeila and Berbera in Africa towards the west. However, these are the vessels of the Asian merchants and we are not informed that any Portugal (or group of Portuguese) sailed with these ships to their appointed destinations.

The respective intelligences of Gaspar Correa, Afonso de Albuquerque and Ruy de Brito must serve as our introduction to the notable embassies of João Coelho and Dom João da Silveira; rendered respectively on behalf of Fernão Peres de Andrade (from Sumatra) and Lopo Soares de Albergaria (from India) for the interests of the Portuguese crown in Asia.

Barros, Decada III Livro II Capitulo III & Capitulo VI
Correa, Tomo I Capitulo X—Armada de Tristão da Cunha
Galvão, pgs. 167, 168, 181, 184

BIBLIOGRAPHY

Printed Sources

1. Barros, João de. *Da Asia*, Vol. 5, Lisbon, 1777.
2. Correa, Gaspar. *Lendas da India*, Lisbon, 1858.
3. Galvão, Antonio. *Tratado dos Descobrimentos*, Porto, Livraria Civilização, 1944.

Published Documents

1. *Cartas de Affonso de Albuquerque*, Tomo I, Lisbon, 1884.
   a) Carta a el-rei de Affonso de Albuquerque—Cananor, November 30, 1513: p. 154, 155. Carta XXX
2. *Cartas de Affonso de Albuquerque*, Tomo III, Lisbon, 1903.
   a) Carta de Ruy de Brito a Affonso de Albuquerque sobre cousas de Malaca—Malacca, January 6, 1514: p. 221.

CHAPTER II   SECTION 2

THE EMBASSY OF JOAM COELHO—1516? AND THE EMBASSY OF DOM JOAM DA SILVEIRA—1518

Lopo Soares de Albergaria, governor of India (1515-1518) in succession to Afonso de Albuquerque (1509-1515), dispatched Dom João da Silveira from Cochin in embassy to the Maldive Islands and the Kingdom of Bengal during 1518. Dom João da Silveira, in a *navio redondo*, sailed as captain-major of an armada of four vessels, with João Fidalgo as captain of a *galeota*, Tristão Barbudo as captain of a *bargantim* and João Moreno as captain of a *caravela*.

Before arrival of the Portuguese fleet at the Maldive Islands, Dom João da Silveira captured two Moorish vessels sailing from Bengal to the Kingdom of Cambay, of which the larger belonged to the Moor Gromalle related to a Moor, the governor of Chatigam (Chittagong) "a principal City of the Kingdom [of] Bengal, being a port by [the] sea, to which respond almost all those things which enter and depart from that Kingdom." (Barros, Decada III Livro II Capitulo III) Dom João da Silveira dispatched the prizes to Cochin and pursued his voyage to the Maldives. Concerning the embassy rendered in the Maldives, and of what Dom João accomplished in the Maldives, these things I hope to inscribe in a later volume. Taking leave of the islands, Dom João da Silveira returned to Cochin for a brief period to replenish his store of provisions, having remained for three months in the Maldive Islands, as Barros records, who, with Castanheda, is the principal source of our intelligence for the establishment of Portuguese relations with the ancient Kingdom of Bengal.

João de Barros records Lopo Soares de Albergaria dispatched Dom João da Silveira to Bengal with petition to the King of Bengal requesting a house for a factory within the realm of Bengal. Castanheda has not elected to notice the return voyage of Dom João to Cochin, but his omission does not impugn the intelligence of Barros, since Castanheda hastens Dom João to Bengal with the utmost dispatch, while Barros, on the contrary, delaying, has chosen to notice some of the particulars of the voyage of Dom João da Silveira where Castanheda keeps his peace.

> "And on the way [to Bengal] he [Dom João da Silveira] was obliged to pass by the Island [of] Ceylon, and the port of Colombo, where our people are accustomed to fetch cinnamon, [where] he could take Pilots to carry him to Bengal, and also [where] secretly he would observe and sound this port [of] Colombo, and the location of the land, for with his opinion, he [Lopo Soares de Albergaria] would determine what they should make, by order of the King, which was a fortress in that place, the captaincy of which would rest with D. João. The said D. João, departing with the four vessels, with which he had sailed to the Maldive Islands, arrived at Colombo, and he saw and observed the place, and took the Pilots, and made his way towards Bengal; and the first port which he took in that bay, which had not yet been discovered by our people, was by the river which

descends from the Kingdom [of] Arakan [presumably a port at (or near) Akyab in modern Burma], where six or seven rowing vessels departed; and after communication with him, they understood he was destined for Bengal, [and] as they were at war with it, they wished to proceed in his company. However Dom João would not allow it, being counseled by a Bengali youth, who he carried, who was [a] brother-in-law of the Pilot of the *nao* which he had captured, saying if he carried those people, as they were hostile to the Bengalis, he would not be well received." (Barros, Decada III Livro II Capitulo III)

Dom João da Silveira and armada arrived before the bar of *Chatigam*—Barros, or *Chetigão*—Castanheda (Chittagong in both instances) on the 9th of May of 1518: being the intelligence of Fernão Lopes de Castanheda. Chittagong is a city well served by water, remarks Castanheda, so that for every road there flows a *ribeiro*-a brook, and the brooks or canals (if that is the interpretation we should give to the word *ribeiro*) are covered by bridges which serve the roads and the *casas terreas*-low lying houses. Both Castanheda and Barros note the large commerce which the city of Chittagong possessed at this time. "It is ruled by a governor called *lascar*[*] by those of the land and he is [a] vassal of the king of Bengal." (Castanheda, Livro IV Capitolo XXXVIII)

The brother-in-law of the pilot of one of the ships Dom João captured enroute to the Maldive Islands, upon arrival at Chittagong, informed the first people to whom he spoke that Dom João had seized those ships, and this matter coming to the attention of the governor of Chittagong, he judged that the Portuguese of the conserve of Dom João da Silveira were pirates. Being however unprepared in his landward defenses, the governor dissimulated with Dom João, until he had attended to the fortification of the city with a trench of two faces, in front of the port, raised with sand and stocked with artillery, erected in the course of one (or several?) nights. Meanwhile the governor entertained (and lulled) Dom João da Silveira with the dispatch of refreshments, requesting peace, which Dom João conceded.

"It happened one day before D. João arrived at port, a *nao* of the land entered it, being of the said port, which came from the City [of] Pacem, which is on the Island [of] Sumatra, loaded with pepper and other kinds of merchandise. In the said *nao* came a Portuguese called João Coelho, that Fernão Peres de Andrade, who was at that port of Pacem freighting for [a voyage to] China, dispatched as [his] messenger on behalf of the King D. Manuel to the King of Bengal, informing him how, being in that port loading a *nao* with pepper, for with it, and others, to come to that City [of] Chatigam [Chittagong] to carry an embassy from the King of Portugal,

---

* From the Persian *sar-i-lashkar*: i.e. commander-in-chief of the forces.

his lord, the principal *nao* of his fleet burned by disaster,[*] as his natives would be able to tell him, who were present, in which the principal things he carried were burned. He asked that in as much as he intended to restore those things which he lost, and thus to send to India for others, which were things of Portugal, he would permit the Portuguese *naos* and *navios* to come to his ports, and that they would be well received, and by this mode other words which he, João Coelho, carried in his instruction." (Barros, Decada III Livro II Capitulo III)

The date of arrival of João Coelho at Bengal is not easily ascertained; not as to the day, or as to the month, at which he arrived at Chittagong, or even as to the year of his disembarkation at that port. Barros appears to suggest that João Coelho arrived at Chittagong a very short time before Dom João da Silveira, or even a single day before Dom João arrived at port, according to the interpretation of the Portuguese of João de Barros—translated in the first sentence of the preceding paragraph—who (and which) is ambiguous. Barros, in any event, appears to assert João Coelho arrived at Chittagong in 1518, unattended as his narrative remains, with a precise statement of that fact. Antonio Galvão, in the *Tratado dos Descobrimentos*, briefly notices the voyages of João Coelho and Dom João da Silveira and asserts the former "was the first Portuguese that I know who drank the water of the River Ganges"; i.e. the first Portuguese to arrive at the Kingdom of Bengal. Galvão assigns the year 1516 as the year of Coelho's arrival. If we accept the date Barros seems to indicate for the arrival of João Coelho at Chittagong, we are obliged to ask why it took Coelho two years to reach Bengal from Sumatra, since Barros indicates Fernão Peres de Andrade dispatched João Coelho from Pacem in 1516. Again if we accept the intelligence of Galvão, one should like to know what João Coelho did for two years at Bengal, since we learn from Barros that Coelho was accredited in embassy to the king of Bengal i.e. Husain Shah (1493-1519), and from the same Barros we learn that João Coelho had not yet rendered his embassy. The respective intelligences of Barros and Galvão present problems of chronology to which I, and all my sources, sifted and digested, are insufficient to the test of a decisive statement, and I leave the question of the arrival-date of João Coelho in Bengal suspended between the years 1516 and 1518, indicating my preference for 1516, since a two year wait upon an oriental monarch seems more palatable than a two year voyage between Pacem and Chittagong. Castanheda is not of any help since he has not condescended to notice the humble João Coelho in any capacity, plunging directly into the military confrontation between Dom João da Silveira and the governor of Chittagong, of which we shall note shortly; nor are Correa and Goes of any assistance to us in the present instance.

---

* The disaster struck the *Belem* which burned on June 2nd 1516 according to a letter contained in the Torre do Tombo (or National Archives of Portugal) at Lisbon, in the collection known as Corpo Cronológico: Parte I Maço 20 Documento 101.

"The said João Coelho, so much as he saw D. João, went to
him presently, innocent of what would happen to him.
D. João, knowing the reason why he came [to Bengal], re-
tained him without leave to return to land, declaring it would
not suit the service of the King for him to go to that business [of the embassy to the king of Bengal], ere he would
damage it, since Fernão Peres was not at that port. And
moreover, he, D. João, had been sent by the Governor Lopo
Soares to dispatch this embassy to the King of Bengal, and
not Fernão Peres, which embassy would be dispatched with
more authority, with some pieces as presents that would be
sent by a person who would go to this. João Coelho being
detained in this manner, the Governor of the City had reason
to be doubly scandalized of D. João, since already he understood how João Coelho came with [a] message to the King
of Bengal, of the part of the King of Portugal by order of his
Captain (according to what all the Bengalis and Moors
would say, who came in the *nao* which carried João Coelho),
they received very good treatment, and he, D. João, had
seized two *naos* which only a short time before had departed
from there, according to what they knew from the Malay
[Bengali?] youth (as we said), so that they affirmed that
Fernão Peres was [the] Captain of the King, and D. João was
some Portuguese turned corsair." (Barros, Decada III Livro
II Capitulo III)

Dom João da Silveira, having anchored before the port of Chittagong, and
now being in need of provisions, requested supplies of the governor in exchange
for his money. The governor replied there were none in the land. Dom João,
knowing the governor lied, and being in need of sustenance, commanded
Tristão Barbudo to seize a *champana* loaded with rice. And thus ensued a
rupture. To the shouts of the people of the *champana* a great number of men
at arms of the city responded to the shore with arrows directed at the Portuguese of Tristão Barbudo, who carried the *champana*, and who perceiving a
great number of people joined in a body, commenced to employ his bombards,
as Castanheda records, and that diligent historian is the sole authority for the
military operations which follow, since Barros has elected to overlook the acts
of war at Chittagong, save in perfunctory notice.

"And as this thing thus was joined, Dom João sent his *batel*
with people and artillery in succor of Tristão Barbudo, and
thus João Fidalgo in his *galeota*, and with their arrival the
fight ignited, in such a manner, that it endured until night,
without any of our people being slayed, but many of the
enemy. From which the Lascar [i.e. governor of Chittagong]
became so incensed that he determined to be revenged upon
them, and presently that night, he arranged to outfit one
hundred *calaluzes* which he had, and before morning he
embarked in them with his people, who would be about five
thousand men the majority of them being archers. And Dom

72

João knowing of the preparations of the enemy, by means of his spies, also prepared for the following day, and obliged the greater part of his people to embark in the *bateis* of his *navio* and *caravela*, and in the *bargantim* and in the *galeota*: and he concerted with João Fidalgo, that arriving the enemy, he would fight them, carrying one hundred and fifty Portuguese for this end, and he would remain in the *navio* and in the *galeota* to come upon them from behind, and fire his artillery if there were need for this, because in this manner he could give greater assistance than going with them to battle." (Castanheda, Livro IV Capitolo XXXVIII)

With the new day the governor of Chittagong departed to attack the fleet of Dom João da Silveira. However the Portuguese artillery commenced to batter the lighter craft of the Moors, and the governor perceiving that his front line was being shattered by the Portuguese guns, and with fear in the vanguard advancing, and as his fleet wanted artillery, the governor rearranged his squadrons in midst of battle, exchanging the rear guard for the van, but to little avail, as the artillery of the Portuguese commanded the seas, notwithstanding the superiority of the Bengalis in point of numbers in men and ships. The Portuguese routed the Moslem fleet with very little effort or loss to themselves: the governor in the van having vainly urged his men to grapple with the Portuguese. The Bengalis fled for shore, suffering numerous losses in dead and injured, with numerous *calaluzes* damaged and others placed on the bottom in a watery grave. The Portuguese did not pursue, as Castanheda instructs, since they were few and the enemy many, but contented themselves with commandeering five *calaluzes*.

"And the Lascar seeing that our people did not pursue, he remained at sea to see what more he could do, and as they [the Portuguese] did nothing more than return to the captain-major, who made great celebration by reason of their victory, and added the five *calaluzes* of the enemy to his armada, and seeing that the war had commenced, he did not wish to remain so near the city, fearing they would be able to set fire to the fleet by night, and deciding to settle near an islet, half a league to the seaward of the city, he dispatched João Fidalgo to that place in his *galeota* to sound it so as to see if it possessed [a] good anchorage. And the Lascar, who was yet at sea, perceiving the *galeota* separate from the body of the fleet, after watching where it went, it appeared to him that he could take it since it was calm, and the flagship and the *caravela* would not be able to succor it, and exerting himself upon this matter, and encouraging his rowers to row with vigor, [and] seeing the *galeota* had almost arrived at the island, he departed from port in great haste with all his fleet *a boga arrācada*-rowing very stoutly, all his people giving a shout with pleasure as though they were in possession of the *galeota*. The captain-major seeing

73

this, presently dispatched the *bargantim,* and two *bateis* to succor it, and as the enemy were exceedingly numerous, they pressed so vigorously that neither by bombard nor by muskets which our people fired could the enemy be kept from arriving at the *galeota* where our people served them with some *panelas de poluora*-pots of gunpowder which they had, but these were so few that presently they were expended, and the enemy entered, not without a stiff fight which our people conducted with spirit and resolution, overturning many of the enemy, but as they were exceedingly numerous compared to our people, they entered injuring all with many shots of the bow. The fight thus continuing, some of the enemy fighting with our people, and others were close to the rudder of the *galeota,* and towing it towards the city, our people yet fighting, Tristão Barbudo and the *bateis* arrived, and they burst upon the enemy like a bolt of lightning, principally Tristão Barbudo who arrived first firing his artillery, and with his people lofting many *panelas de poluora*-pots of gunpowder at the *calaluzes* of the enemy which presently commenced to burn and the enemy with fear jumped into the sea. By means of this artifice in [a] very short time they cleared the *galeota* of the foe who had enclosed it, and as João Fidalgo and his people had only to contend with the enemy in the *galeota,* they soon cleared them from it, [some] jumping into the sea with fear, while the ship remained full of many others who our people had slayed, and Our Lord approved that none of our people died, neither then or afterwards from the many injuries which all possessed. The *galeota* having been cleared, and in a body with the *bargantim* and *bateis,* routed the enemy who fled for the city, and passing in front of the flagship and the *caravela,* they were greeted by the play of bombards, and thus they returned to port with numerous *calaluzes* burnt, and placed on the bottom, and [with] many dead and injured people." (Castanheda, Livro IV Capitolo XXXVIII)

States of peace and war alternately attended the passions of the captains of both parties during the rainy season on that coast. Hope, fear and anger animated the breast of Dom João da Silveira, but hunger stalked the body of every Portugal. The wind and rain of the southwest Monsoon battered the fleet, while Dom João could secure provisions from a hostile shore only with the greatest of difficulties, and the captain-major had no remedy other than to remain on that coast. As João de Barros notes Dom João was obliged to drink the works of iron, fire and famine, or shed his life.

Barros records an instance in which Dom João da Silveira and his conserve were suffering from extreme hunger when the governor of Chittagong—of a sudden—decided to settle peace with the Portuguese. His reason: he expected certain ships at port and feared Dom João would seize them. Dom João then released João Coelho, the ambassador of Fernão Peres de Andrade, accredited to the court of Bengal, who, according to Barros, gave Dom João da Silveira life by reason of the provisions which he obtained for the Portuguese at this time; thus from certain friends of his, dispatched secretly by night, and by day with the consent of the governor. And when the ships arrived, and discharged their wares, the governor of Chittagong returned to wage war once again. Dom João da Silveira, however, suffered more from the effects of hunger and the sodden monsoon than from the concentrated enmity of his malign foes and the impact of their feeble iron against his flesh.

Tristão Barbudo, to return to Castanheda, was enjoined to burn certain rafts which the Bengalis intended to employ as vehicles of fire against the armada of Dom João da Silveira. Ascending the river of Chittagong (i.e. the Karnafuli River) towards port—after Dom João and fleet had dropped down river towards the bar—Tristão Barbudo failed to discover the rafts, and falling down river with his *bargantim*, and being within sight of the captain-major, Tristão Barbudo was approached by five *lancharas* of the enemy conveying three hundred archers. Fearful for the safety of Tristão Barbudo, Dom João dispatched Gaspar Fernandes *cavaleiro fidalgo*, a resident of the little town of Pombal, in his *batel* with fifteen Portuguese to assist Tristão Barbudo. Gaspar Fernandes discharged his commission with spirit and courage. This redoubtable Portugal with his intrepid companions attacked and boarded the lead *lanchara*, slaying the enemy, and forcing others to leap into the sea.

Gaspar Fernandes returned to the *batel*, with his men, and with the same band of warriors, he rushed at a second *lanchara* nearby, but the Moors did not care to encounter Gaspar Fernandes, and beached the *lanchara* on the shore, and with bow and arrow wrought more damage upon land than they had at sea, and Castanheda, who records the combat of Gaspar Fernandes with the five *lancharas*, asserts Gaspar Fernandes and his little band sustained many arrow wounds, but undaunted, Gaspar Fernandes returned to attack the three remaining *lancharas*, that Tristão Barbudo had been entertaining to the tune of his bombards. When the three *lancharas* observed the approach of the *batel*, and understanding the defeat of their companions, they refused to await the onset of the terrible Gaspar Fernandes and fled with the utmost dispatch, although all the Portuguese were severely injured, including the captain of the *batel* who sustained a leg wound from an arrow-shot. A son of Gaspar Fernandes died, and perhaps others. Having routed the enemy, Gaspar Fernandes returned to the conserve of Dom João da Silveira before whose eyes this deed had been wrought, carrying the *lanchara* captured from the enemy.

João Coelho, it appears, rendered his embassy to the king of Bengal (i.e. to Husain Shah, 1493-1519) not long after his release by Dom João da Silveira. Having recourse to the pages of João de Barros we learn that *circa* the time of his release, a message arrived from the king of Bengal, to the governor of Chittagong, asking that João Coelho would now come. We have noted that the Bengalis considered João Coelho the ambassador of the king of Portugal, and Dom João, and all his companions, as pirates who had revolted from the king of Portugal, and were therefore equally enemies of Portugal and Bengal. João Coelho, to the contrary, was considered as a friend, and treated with consideration and respect, by reason of the good treatment which the Moslem merchants received from the hands of Fernão Peres de Andrade when he was at Pacem in the island of Sumatra.

Undoubtedly João Coelho rendered his embassy at Gaur, the old capital of Bengal (near modern English Bazar) and undoubtedly João Coelho ascended the Ganges River to wait on King Husain Shah of Bengal, and thus rendered his embassy on behalf of Fernão Peres de Andrade, and his lord, King Manuel I of Portugal, but no historian has elected to reveal any of the particulars of his embassy and peregrination, save João de Barros, who asserts João Coelho was called, and notes his intention to return to Portuguese India, having rendered his embassy, and Antonio Galvão, who declares João Coelho was the first Portuguese to drink the water of the Ganges.*

The governor of Chittagong now sought his revenge against Dom João da Silveira, João Fidalgo, Tristão Barbudo, Gaspar Fernandes and their formidable company by means of ruse rather than by main force, as his feeble military instrument had proved insufficient to every test.

> "He [the governor of Chittagong] plotted with the King of
> Arakan, a vassal at that time of the King of Bengal, who
> inhabited a City of this name, about fifteen leagues from the
> mouth of a river, and thirty-five leagues from the port of
> Chatigam [Chittagong]; these things being settled, a few
> days afterwards a well-dressed man came to D. João from that
> place, accompanied by people in three or four rowing-craft;
> he presented to him a valuable ruby on behalf of the King
> of Arakan, placed in a ring, saying that he [the king] knew
> how he was out of sorts with the people of Chittagong, be-
> cause of the evil treatment which he received from them,
> and he greatly desired to have friendship and commerce
> with the Portuguese, by the good fame which they pos-
> sessed in those parts, [and thus] he had been sent to visit
> him, asking that he would be pleased to come to the port
> of his City [of] Arakan, where he would be provided with
> whatever he needed. D. João received the present, thanking
> the Ambassador by giving him some things. He [i.e. Dom
> João also] communicated with the principals of the fleet.
> And with the work and danger which had passed at that
> port, and the need in which he remained for provision
> [being at the end of winter—Castanheda], so as to be able
> to navigate, because the waters of winter, which in that place
> is very severe, had rotted his rigging and the sails of the
> ships, so that now he was served by some of cotton, which
> they made from [the] nets of some fishermen which they

---

* But cf. Appendix II. I believe the first paragraph of that letter, the said letter being unpublished, refers to the visit of João Coelho to Gaur, the capital of Bengal, but alas, this document does not admit of a decisive statement.

assaulted,[*] he decided that it would be best to go to the port of Arakan, of which he already had intelligence how it was a well-supplied City, and [one] with trade." (Barros, Decada III Livro II Capitulo III)

We shall follow the armada of Dom João da Silveira to the Kingdom of Arakan in Chapter III with very little delay.

---

* "And [Dom João da Silveira] seeing his fleet without shrouds and stays and that he could not navigate [without them] arranged to take so many nets from a nearby village of fishermen, and from them he arranged to have cords made on land for the shrouds and stays. And being at this [work], the Lascar came with many people to obstruct it, and a great fight ensued between our people and the enemy. And after this peace returned between the Lascar, and Dom João, who would not trust him without hostages, and being delivered, he returned to the port [of Chittagong], at which he remained for fifteen days trading." (Castanheda, Livro IV Capitolo XXXVIII)

Barros, Decada III Livro II Capitulo III & Capitulo VI
Castanheda, Livro IV Capitolo XXXII, Capitolo XXXV, Capitolo XXXVII, Capitolo XXXVIII & Capitolo XXXIX
Correa, Tomo II Capitulo XIII, Capitulo XV & Capitulo XVI—Lenda de Lopo Soares
Galvão, pgs. 181, 184
Goes, Parte IV Capitulo XXVII

BIBLIOGRAPHY
PRINTED SOURCES

1. Barros, João de. *Da Asia*, Vol. 5, Lisbon, 1777.
2. Castanheda, Fernão Lopes de. *História do Descobrimento & Conquista da India pelos Portugueses*, Coimbra, Imprensa da Universidade, 1928.
3. Correa, Gaspar. *Lendas da India*, Lisbon, 1860.
4. Galvão, Antonio. *Tratado dos Descobrimentos*, Porto, Livraria Civilização, 1944.
5. Goes, Damião de. *Crónica do Felicissimo Rei D. Manuel*, Coimbra, Imprensa da Universidade, 1926.

DOCUMENTS

1. Letter of Simão de Seixas to the King D. Manuel—Pacem, September 20, 1516. Corpo Cronológico: Parte I Maço 20 Documento 101.
2. Letter of Dom João de Lima to the King D. Manuel—Cochin, December 22, 1518. Corpo Cronológico: Parte I Maço 23 Documento 117.
3. Letter of the King of Bengal to the King of Portugal—The City of Bengal (i.e. Gaur), without date. Cartas dos Vice-reis: Número 108.

CHAPTER II   SECTION 3

THE RETURN VOYAGE OF DOM FRANCISCO DE TRAVAMQUA— 1518-1519

Antonio de Miranda de Azevedo declares that a *fusta* (i.e. a pinnace) returned to the coast of Bengal after Dom João da Silveira departed from the shores of that Bay (i.e. after his voyages to Bengal and Arakan).

EXTRACT OF THE LETTER OF ANTONIO DE MIRANDA DE AZEVEDO TO THE KING D. MANUEL
Dated the Fortress of Santa Barbara,
on the Island of Ceylon, 8th November 1519

"Your Highness will know that after Lopo Soares departed from here [in December 1518], it appeared well to Dom João [da Silveira, first captain of the fortress at Colombo, 1518-1519] that with two *fustas* I should run the ports and rivers of this island to oblige the *naos* and *champanas* to come, who, out of fear of us, have ceased to come to this port. For this reason I went and gave *seguros*-passes to them and I made them come. When I wanted to return I found the wind so great that I was driven by force to the Maldive Islands where I found a *fusta* which had gone to Bengal with Dom João.[*] And when it came the men of arms revolted against the captain, and they made another tumult at night, so that Dom João had them for lost. They elected Dom Francisco, son of Dom João de Travamqua, as their captain, and they returned to the coast of Bengal with the intention of seizing everything they found. They came to the Maldive Islands in February [of 1519] three days before I [arrived]. When they saw me they put themselves in arms against me, but I, Lord, had with them such manner, that they had for better counsel to deliver the *fusta* to me." (*As Gavetas da Torre do Tombo*, Vol. IV, 1519—Novembro 8 Letter of Antonio de Miranda de Azevedo to the King— Ceylon)

---

* The intelligence of the *fusta* is difficult to reconcile with the notices of Barros, Castanheda and Goes, all of whom assert Dom João da Silveira departed for Bengal with four vessels. Castanheda states these were a *navio redondo*, a *galeota*, a *bargantim* and a *caravela*. Perhaps the *fusta* joined Dom João da Silveira en route, or after he arrived at Bengal. (*Quamdo me tornava achey tamto vemto que por força m' esguarou as Ilhas de Maldiva homde achey huma fusta que com Dom João fora a Bemgalla,* in the Portuguese of Antonio de Miranda de Azevedo)

78

THE VOYAGE OF RAFAEL PERESTRELLO—1521-1523?

The governor of India, Diogo Lopes de Sequeira (1518-1521), dispatched Rafael Perestrello from the port of Diu to sail to Bengal on a commercial venture. Rafael Perestrello departed from Cochin in April (or May) of 1521, apparently in the fleet of Jorge de Albuquerque, the new captain of Malacca, who had been charged by the governor with securing possession of the port of Pacem, on the island of Sumatra, en route to Malacca, and there to place on the throne of that city-state a client prince, whose father had lost his throne (and life) in a revolt; while the prince had fled to India seeking to be restored to his inheritance by the Portuguese. More importantly, Jorge de Albuquerque was instructed to raise a fortress at Pacem.

Rafael Perestrello loaded his *nao* with pepper at Pacem, and with other commodities useful for the purposes of trade at Bengal, and as the monsoon for Bengal had not yet arrived, he waited for it, while Jorge de Albuquerque, after erecting the fortress at Pacem, sailed to Malacca. Rafael Perestrello made his way to Bengal where he arrived at the port of Chatigam (Chittagong) in safety, ca. August-September 1521, passing the islands of Andramu (Andaman?) where he nearly went to wreck.

Of the relevant particulars of the stay of Rafael Perestrello at the Kingdom of Bengal there remain but a few meagre scraps, discovered principally amongst the pages of João de Barros.

Scrap #1—While at Bengal Rafael Perestrello had by means of one Alle Aga (Ali Aga) fifteen survivors of the wreck of a Portuguese vessel which sank between the Maldive Islands and the coast of Sumatra, and they, in a *batel*, had gone to the Kingdom of Pegu.

Scrap #2—Dom Andre Anriques, the captain of Pacem (1522-1523), dispatched Jeronymo de Sorande in a Bengali *nao* to Rafael Perestrello with letters in 1522, asking him to dispatch a junk loaded with provisions for his need (the Portuguese were at war with the king of Acheh). Rafael Perestrello complied with the request of Dom Andre by dispatching Domingos de Seixas, scrivener of his *nao*, in the *navio* of Gaspar Ferraz who had arrived in Bengal by the road of commerce; apparently in the year of 1522. Domingos de Seixas never reached Dom Andre, because sailing to the city of Tenaçarij (Tenasserim), from Chittagong, to obtain the provisions which Dom Andre sought, he was imprisoned by the governor of the city, and with sixteen Portugals with him, was carried to the king of Siam (i.e. to Rama T'ibodi II, 1491-1529) where he remained a prisoner for twenty-five years.*

---

* Domingos de Seixas after some years as a prisoner in Siam became a captain of "men at arms" in the Siamese army, with great liberties, and who—in the wars of the kings of Siam—traversed great reaches of Siam and neighboring lands. João de Barros acknowledges him as the principal source of his intelligence relating to the geography and customs of the Siamese nation, of which Barros speaks at length as we noted in *The First Age of the Portuguese Embassies, Navigations and Peregrinations to the Kingdoms and Islands of Southeast Asia (1509-1521)*.

Scrap #3—We are informed, being Rafael Perestrello at Bengal, a *navio* came to Chittagong with as many as fifty men aboard, not as merchants, but as pirates having revolted against the authority of the governor of India. This vessel came from Coromandel, plundering the ships of the Moors: Captain one Diogo Gago, and arrived at Bengal in 1522 or 1523, where Rafael Perestrello tried to remove Diogo Gago and ruffians from their evil persuasion, but to no result. This vessel sailed from Chittagong to Tenasserim. Before arrival at port, Balthazar Veloso, with the assistance of João Barbudo, murdered the captain by stabbing him to death while he lay asleep on the lap of his slave girl. Arriving at Tenasserim, Simão de Brito having been elected for captain, the *navio* robbed a great *champana* at (or near) Tenasserim, while Domingos was yet at port. The governor of the city had his revenge, not against Simão de Brito, and his unsavory company, but against the innocent Domingos de Seixas, and the Portuguese with him, who were carried prisoners to King Rama T'ibodi II of Siam.

Barros, Decada III Livro IV Capitulo X; Livro V Capitulo I, Capitulo II & Capitulo III; Livro VIII Capitulo II

We shall have further occasion to note the things of Rafael Perestrello, still in perfunctory notice, when we speak of the embassy of Gonçalo Tavares in Chapter II Section 6, exchanging João de Barros, at that time, for the anonymous author of the narrative of his embassy to the court of Bengal.

BIBLIOGRAPHY
PRINTED SOURCES

1. Barros, João de. *Da Asia*, Vols. 5 & 6, Lisbon, 1777.

CHAPTER II   SECTION 5

THE VOYAGE OF ANTONIO DE BRITO *O VELHO*—1521

In the year in which Rafael Perestrello sailed to Bengal we are informed by Gaspar Correa that Diogo Lopes de Sequeira dispatched Antonio de Brito *o velho* (the old man) in a *nao* to the Kingdom of Bengal, via Pacem. Barros refers to Antonio de Brito and records he went to Bengal with an armada. The notices of Correa and Barros are thus sufficiently meagre in the extreme.

Barros, Decada III Livro VIII Capitulo III
Correa, Tomo II Capitulo XIII & Capitulo XVI—Lenda de Diogo Lopes de Sequeira

BIBLIOGRAPHY
PRINTED SOURCES

1. Barros, João de. *Da Asia*, Vol. 6, Lisbon, 1777.
2. Correa, Gaspar. *Lendas da India*, Lisbon, 1860.

THE EMBASSY OF GONSALO TAVARES TO THE COURT OF BENGAL, DISPATCHED BY ANTONIO DE BRITO *O VELHO* FROM THE PORT OF CHITTAGONG ON OCTOBER 13TH 1521

The meagre intelligence of Gaspar Correa and João de Barros upon the voyage of Antonio de Brito to Bengal is supplemented by intelligence derived from a 16th century manuscript: *Lembrança dalgumas coussas que se passaram quando Amtonio de Bryto e Dyogo Pereyra foram a Bemgalla asy em Bengala como em Tanaçaiym e em Pegu onde tambem fomos* (Remembrance of some things which happened when Antonio de Brito and Diogo Pereira went to Bengal, thus in Bengal, as in Tenasserim, and in Pegu, where also we went) found in a collection of the Torre do Tombo entitled *São Vicente*, but more importantly—for our own purposes—we are able to narrate at great length an embassy dispatched from the city of Chatigam (Chittagong) to the court of the king of Bengal, at Gaur, led by Gonçalo Tavares, and with whom the anonymous author of our manuscript journeyed, and from this same manuscript I propose to narrate the particulars of this embassy, as the printed sources of the sixteenth century Portugals have not noticed it, and because this manuscript has not yet been published, and is very little known.

The anonymous author of our manuscript commences his account of the Portuguese embassy to the city of Bengal by noting his entourage departed Chittagong on October 13th 1521, and by means of this notice we understand that Antonio de Brito *o velho* had arrived at the port of Chittagong—from Pacem. The embassy travelled by horseback with horses given to the Portuguese for this purpose, to a place called Aluia,* six leagues from Chittagong, where the embassy arrived that night, and where the Portuguese discovered their personal effects (*fato*), which had been dispatched ahead of them by sea, had arrived, and at this place the embassy was lodged in the best dilapidated houses (*pardyejros*) that the town possessed, "because all the houses are such." Here the Portuguese remained for fifteen days "without seeing [a] person of good aspect with whom we could speak," whence being bored, the members of the embassy departed at times to see the surrounding countryside. Our author records that Aluia lay on a river which entered the land for a distance of two leagues, and upon this river were sheltered many rowing-vessels and ships of cargo, which at low tide were stranded, and at high tide the quantity of water that entered was such, that a *nao* of three hundred tons might be floated. The town of Aluia was (and perhaps still is) situated in a pleasant countryside, with many groves of trees possessing many fruits, alas different from those known to Portugal, and the lands of Aluia are applied to the culture of rice and sugar.

At the term of the said fifteen days an eunuch with the name of Alla arrived. He brought seven well-equipped *quystes* which "are some rowing-vessels which in these parts we call *bragamtys*" to fetch the embassy, and the next day (*a outro dya segymte*) the Portuguese and Bengali entourage departed to proceed to the king of Bengal one hundred and forty-five leagues in the interior of the country, and as our author declares, the first forty-five leagues

---

* Perhaps near modern Sitakund; or yet upon the Fenny River?

are strewn with a great sum of islands and sandbars, some of which are readily perceived, others less so, and as the author of our manuscript avers, many of these islands were in former times inhabitated, but by reason of the force of the seasons and great currents in these parts, the chief part have been inundated.

No sooner had the entourage departed than they experienced a disaster due to the great force of the incoming tide which overturned three *quystes*, in which one hundred and thirty-five people (apparently all Bengalis) perished, and caused the said *quystes* to be broken in pieces, and that day after sunset the entourage arrived at an island called Zogydya,* nine or ten leagues from Aluia. Thence it remained that night and the following day, and at eight o'clock the next morning it departed from Zogydya and arrived the following evening, toward sunset, at another island called Guacalla,** and upon the way our author declares the embassy saw two small islands with groves of trees and other islands that were flat with sand "and we asked what land that was, and they told us that this land had been peopled in former days, and with the great tempests and great currents, all had been consumed, and now it was of that fashion."

The Portuguese remained at Guacalla for three days since the weather was unfit for travel and because the eunuch, Alla, was temporarily ill. During this time the Portuguese had occasion to proceed by land to look at some of the things that the land possessed (*teuemos luguar damdar pela tera a ver allgumas coussas das que nela ha*) among which our author declares the Portuguese saw a great monastery of God (*mesteiro de deus*), a crippled man who could tie a fagot with his fingernail and many cloths of the land. Before departure from Guacalla, the Portuguese searched for some contrivance by which to convey one Pedro Tavares to Chittagong, who was so sick the Portuguese had great fear for his life, "and God was willing that we found a *parao* in which we sent him for which Gonçalo Tavares [evidently his relation] paid eleven *tangas* for his conveyance to Chatigam [Chittagong] and his departure caused us great grief since we did not know if they would carry him safely."

When the Portuguese and Bengali party had departed this island of Guacalla (after a stay of three or four days) they proceeded by *quystes* close to land and when the sun had nearly set, the entourage was attacked by a band of robbers in three *quystes* who caused the seven *quystes* of the Bengalis, conveying the Portuguese embassy, to take flight upon their approach—leaving the Portugals in a snare (*laço*). But God willed, in the words of our author, that the Portuguese came to land ahead of the robbers, being an island called Meamgare (unidentified) described by our author as a very pleasant land of many cloths. The people of the land are civil and do not bear arms, and the island is three leagues long and two and one-half leagues in width. In this island the Portuguese departed by land with some *negros* to carry their personal effects (*fato*) on their backs since the sea was infested with numerous *quystes* of robbers, and

---

* At the town of Jugdea, halfway between Noakhali and the mouth of the Fenny River, the British possessed a factory in the days of the East India Company. Zogydya, described as an island, is perhaps located here, or opposite Jugdea at (or upon) one of the islands that lie across the Bamni.

** Localized near modern Dakhin Shahbazpur Island.

the *quystes* that had so recently fled in disgrace, proceeded by sea upon the other side of the island without cargo and hence the embassy departed by the river that would take them to the king of Bengal.

> "And upon the way from this land [of Meamgare], as far as the river, we saw two very great islands, and [they were] very beautifully wooded, in which they told us there were many wild elephants, and the islands are uninhabited, and before we arrived at the end of this river, we found four *paraos* of robbers, and they were upon land having something to eat, and the *paraos* were full of taut canes on end similar to lances. These are the best arms which they have.
>
> "And we entered by the river inside and that first night we slept at the foot of a tree because there was no other place at which one might lodge, and thus we proceeded by the river [for] five days, and we saw from one side, as from the other, many little places, and among them no hackney horses were to be found, and along this river are many fields of sugar where a great deal of very fine sugar is gathered, and it is free for the taking. This is what we perceived in these five days and at the end of these days we arrived at a city called Noamalaquo." *

As the Portuguese arrived at night, they slept in the *quyste*, and the next day (*ao outro dya*) the Portuguese went ashore, whence the bailiff (*meyrynho*) of the land presently came and offered them a lodging to share with livestock sheltered there at night, and which was a building open at all the sides, covered by a roof of thatch, and with a floor upon which the Portuguese were desired to repose amid great piles of manure. "We said to them that they could keep such a lodging for themselves, that we should lodge in the *quyste* since we were accustomed to the sea." Thereupon a message was dispatched to the governor (*regedor*) of the city, Abarcam (*Abar* Khan), upon this matter of the lodgings, and he granted the Portuguese a good lodging (*boa poussada*), and after the

---

* On the map of João Baptista Lavanha, who edited Decada IV of João de Barros, after his death, and published his notes in 1615 (*editio princeps*) with a map of Bengal, among others, are situated two towns, Noldij and Cuipitauas, immediately south of a town called Naomoluco, which is itself due south of another called Maluco. H. Blochmann, in a learned monograph entitled "Contributions to the Geography and History of Bengal (Muhammadan Period)," *Journal of the Asiatic Society of Bengal*, Calcutta, 1873, identifies Cuipitauas with Khalifatabad (in the environs of Bagherhat) and Noldy with Noldi on the Nabaganga, east of Jessore, near the Madhumati River. If these identifications are just, we ought to look for Noamalaquo (or Noamaluquo, as it is spelled in a different part of our manuscript), which is either the Naomoluco or Maluco of the map of João Baptista Lavanha, somewhere near the modern town of Kushtia. The embassy of Gonçalo Tavares, it appears, entered that part of Bengal called Bakarganj and ascended the line of the Madhumati to a point near the present town of Kushtia.

Portuguese were settled, the governor called, and our author relates that he went presently to see what he wanted.

> "Arriving at the door, the said houses [of the governor] appeared to me to be three hundred paces around, and next to one of the sides, was a very great fosse, and it was full of water and was fashioned of *taypa*-stucco. At the first door were eight men all bearing *treçados*-broad swords at the waist and with some great canes in their hands, and the second enclosure was made of brick after our manner, and at the door of this enclosure were twenty men who guarded it, and inside were many people, and beyond this door was an audience hall. The partition was of brick."

At this interview the governor of the city desired to know what the Portuguese wished, and what they had brought him in the way of presents. Our author responded that they brought nothing more than what they had given at Chittagong. The governor replied that he was king in that land and that he possessed the power to kill our author, or to give him life, to which our author responded that he well understood all, but that it was the duty of the governor to treat the Portuguese with great respect since the king of Bengal would desire it, and that such words were unbecoming of such a great lord, and other words of like admonition, to which the author of our manuscript responded to the menaces of the man within whose power he remained. When our author finished, the governor laughed, embraced him, and declared that he spoke the truth and dispatched him with presents of some livestock and fruits of the land, and thus our author took leave of the governor and returned to Gonçalo Tavares.

For twenty days the Portuguese waited for word of their dispatch to the court of Bengal, and not having it, our author again returned to the governor to ask him to dispatch the embassy as quickly as possible so the Portuguese *naos* (i.e. the ships of the conserve of Antonio de Brito at Chittagong) would not sustain any loss. The governor rebutted the more he was nettled, the worse he would be served, and the governor terminated the interview in an abrupt manner, leaving his guest alone, whence the latter went for his lodgings, and upon the way our author "encountered a man of Cristovão Jussarte, and speaking with him, I asked about Cristovão Jussarte, and what dispatch they had to proceed to the house of the King, and thus speaking we arrived to where Cristovão Jussarte was." From this statement, and from others that follow in our manuscript, we understand that the Portuguese were not only well-established in the Kingdom of Bengal in this year of 1521, but were yet established in the interior of the said kingdom, as we shall have occasion to notice once again with the arrival of the embassy of Gonçalo Tavares at Gaur, and from the above statement it appears that Cristovão Jussarte had preceded Gonçalo Tavares to the court of the king of *Bengala*.

Cristovão Jussarte desired to know what purpose his countrymen had in mind in coming to Noamalaquo, and when he knew of their embassy, he declared to our author that the Portuguese of Gonçalo Tavares were greatly deceived and that all would be as he, Cristovão Jussarte, would wish and that he would aid the Portuguese to fetch a cargo of merchandise. Our author replied that Gonçalo Tavares and his entourage had not come so far to trade, but to serve the king, their lord, and that both Cristovão Jussarte and Gonçalo Tavares knew what pertained to the king's service, and thus our author spoke other words, following which he returned to Gonçalo Tavares. Gonçalo Tavares, however, asked our author to return to Cristovão Jussarte with some letters of Rafael Perestrello (who, as we noted in Chapter II Section 4, had sailed to Chittagong) and of one Duarte Rodrigues, and to ask the pardon of Cristovão Jussarte for not coming to see him directly because he was a little ill and abused by the journey, and that feeling better, he would come to speak with him.

Our author relates that he arrived at the house of Cristovão Jussarte, and did as Gonçalo Tavares had directed, and informed Cristovão Jussarte that as soon as Gonçalo Tavares felt better he would come to speak to him on how to best concert this embassy, and to come to some accord upon it.

> "And the said Cristovão Jussarte read the letters, and when he read some of Antonio de Brito, he swore at God for such a stupid man as was Rafael Perestrello who had taken his flag, and that he had left it there for Antonio de Brito; that if he had been there, such a thing would not have been permitted,[*] and thus he said so many other things in so base a manner that they are not fit to write and I desired to be gone from him so as not to hear more; he told me to tell Gonçalo Tavares not to speak with the governor, or with any other person, without speaking to him first."

Notwithstanding the very partial and ill-mannered advice of Cristovão Jussarte, our author relates that the Portuguese of his embassy went again *ao outro dya seguymte* to speak to the governor who had ordered them to bring the present they intended for the king of Bengal, and after seeing it, he dispatched the Portuguese with two goats for their sustenance. Following this interview the Portuguese (some or all) proceeded to the house of Cristovão Jussarte where they spoke upon many things. From what our author records we divine that the purpose of this embassy was to settle peace with the Kingdom of Bengal so as to provide the fortresses of Malacca and Pacem (the latter being constructed only in this year of 1521) with a source of secure purveyance. Moreover Cristovão Jussarte, we learn, sought to dissuade Gonçalo Tavares from visiting the king of Bengal in embassy, saying he was merely doing the bidding of Antonio de Brito, and that he could neither expect honor or profit in this enterprise, nor was such a visit necessary, all without result.

En route to their lodgings the company of Gonçalo Tavares encountered one Gromalle "which means captain" ** come from the king of Bengal, who they asked for their dispatch. The Portuguese knew the said Gromalle had been dis-

---

* We are only left to surmise the meaning and circumstances of this incident of the flag.

** From the Persian *sharabdar-i-ghair-mahalli*: i.e. captain of the goblet beyond the palace. This title appears on a Bengali inscription dated A.H. 918 (A.D. 1512-1513). Vide H. Blochmann: "Notes on Arabic and Persian Inscriptions," *Journal of the Asiatic Society of Bengal*, Calcutta, 1872, and Momtazur Rahman Tarafdur: *Husain Shahi Bengal*, Dacca, 1965, p. 95, 96.

patched to oblige the governor (*regedor*) to proceed to court "since it appeared to the king that he desired to flee," and because the king of Bengal desired to know the truth of the Portuguese of the conserve of Gonçalo Tavares, since his bailiff (*algozyll*) had written to him that they were robbers and deceivers who came to spy the land, and afterwards to seize it, for which the Gromalle had taken an oath declaring he would inform the king truly upon this matter. The Gromalle declared he would do all he could to see that the Portuguese embassy was dispatched promptly. The Portuguese apparently saw the governor once again this day upon matters of their dispatch, and the following day (*ao outro dya segymte*) but again to no avail.

"And we were in this place [for an additional?] fifteen days without having any dispatch, and, because at times we were bored, we journeyed through this city for our diversion and so as to be able to give credence to certain things.

"And without benefit of the labor of man the land is very pleasant in all things, save waters, which are very bad. This [is] because all are stagnant and they are of the manner that I will give notice. The land has many palm groves and [it is situated] between these groves of palms and all is made into great and very long pools, and between these pools the houses are placed so that all the houses have water at the door and [the people] bathe themselves in these pools and for these reasons the houses are bad and [the] waters [likewise].

"In the land there are many black and white cloths and many market stalls. These black cloths are twelve ells [in length] and five in width, and in this place there are some *beatylhas*-muslin cloths eight ells [in length] and four and one-half in width and they are checkered with some bands of silk being a hand's breadth at the ends. Thus it is with silk, and thus there are others, of many diverse manners, and they are very inexpensive, and in the same land there are some cloths of cotton like *resposteyros*-drapes, and they are very inexpensive, and here there are great supplies of very inexpensive *manteigas*-butters and very inexpensive and white sugar."

At the end of the said fifteen days, the Portuguese were embarked with intent to proceed upon their journey to the court of Bengal, and moreover were embarked for three days without benefit of departure from Noamalaquo, and at the end of the said three days, Gonçalo Tavares sent our author to the governor to know why the Portuguese were not permitted to depart. The scurrilous governor showed great anger "saying we were some dogs and that we were never content, and when I saw this, without saying more, I proceeded to the *paraos*, and when he saw that I was angry, he gave us our dispatch."

The Portuguese, including Cristovão Jussarte, were carried a league and a half to a strait that contained some very high reeds covering it, and which swarmed with *mosquytos*. The Portuguese wanted food or counsel from the Bengalis who accompanied them and when they saw this, they asked "those *negros*" to be gone. The Bengalis excused themselves, declaring they awaited the bailiff (*agoazyll*), who would arrive in eight days. Without hope and without counsel, the Portuguese in despair had means whereby the *negros* were obliged to jump into the sea, and the Portuguese, oars in hand, crossed to the other side of the strait and tied the *paraos* to some jetties. The following day (*a outro dya*) Cristovão Jussarte dispatched a Portugal by land to the king of Bengal. He arrived safely at Gaur but did not speak with the king. We are not given his name.

The *negros* returned to the governor and related these things to him and the governor, angered by their neglect, ordered the principal members of their company tied hand and foot, and then released them, directing the *negros* to return to the Portuguese, and not to allow the ambassadorial party to proceed for more than two leagues each day, and thus the *negros* did as they were directed, and in the space of ten days the Portuguese had proceeded only eighteen leagues.

"Along this river we saw many things of which I do not write, as they would be prolix, among which we saw some great *naos* with poops after the manner of our ships, and the prows are similar to those of the *caravelas latynas* and they do not have any masts and all are covered so that the rain does not enter. The rudders are like those of the *caravelas latynas*, and they are very wide upon the bottom and require very little depth, and they load with great quantities of rice, and some of them are so large that they load one thousand *camdys*, and they sail always by tow and they have this manner of towing.

"From the *nao* to land [there is] a cable on barks, and landward upon the point of this cable are fastened so many links for as many men as are needed, so that each man carries his link, and beyond are seven or eight men who have care of [how] they carry it. They attach the links to some things, and moreover [this is done] for the purpose of striking them from the prows of the *naos*. They have a deck with a castle after the manner of our *naos*, in which castle are seven or eight men—according to the [size of the] *nao*—and they carry in their *naos* some great canes, six or seven *braças*-fathoms long in order to favor the *nao* when it veers for land, and moreover they have some great shelters in which they turn [the ships] about by canes since they are unable to control them [otherwise] by reason of the great quantity of water, and if they chance to run aground they are broken in a thousand pieces because they are very thinly planked and lack joining.

"The river is of this fashion. It is as wide as from Almada to Lisbon and there are sites in the middle of it. There are many sandbars and the water flows so swiftly and runs to the shallowest places, that *toqueys*-rotten spots are carved touching the *costado*-ship's sides with land, and you do not find bottom with five or six *braças*-fathoms, and sometimes, if you are not careful in your bark, a great piece of earth comes tumbling down which buries whoever proceeds below, and this is because above [there is] grit and below ooze, and it now flows with such force, and the water steals it from below in such a manner that it does this. This is what we saw on the river."

Perceiving these things on the Ganges, and others, as our author declares, the Portuguese arrived at a place called Meinatepur (unidentified) where they remained for three days, being told the bailiff (*algoazyll*) would come. At the end of the said three days Cristovão Jussarte departed by land with the *fato* and "the *negros* raised hand upon it in such a fashion that they made a very great commotion." The *algozyll*, having arrived at this time, fetched both Cristovão Jussarte and the *fato*, and the next day (*hao outro dya*) the Portuguese departed once again and that night they slept at a place called Moulana Damga (unidentified) where they found many inexpensive cloths of silk for sale, and moreover they knew the land possessed a great deal of iron and that the *bar* was worth three *pardaos*.

"And from that place we departed and in three days we arrived in the afternoon at Garell [Gaur]. On the riverbank we saw so many *paraos*, of such divers manners, that I do not know how to relate it, among which I counted one hundred and thirty all ornamented in gold, and I asked whose *paraos* they were, and they told me that they were of the person of the king.

"We saw a *nao* which carried the governor of Sornagam [Sonargaon] to give service to the King, which was of this manner; the poop was round with its chambers all ornamented in gold, and in the middle of it was a *curucheo*-spire, likewise of gold, and inside it was wrought with gold and azure with [a] thousand figures. It was chiselled, and round, with balconies, and thus gilded, and beneath the balconies were some balconies and removables after the manner of a *galeam*-printer's galley upon which rowed two hundred oarsmen, and its prow was similar to that of a *caravela* with its cutwater, and all [the] body of the *nao* wanting gold, was painted in divers colors."

When the Portuguese arrived at Garell (Gaur), the governor (*regedor*) of the city arranged to lodge them in his house, but when Cristovão Jussarte knew of this, he expressed his displeasure to the governor, saying he did not care to inhabit the same house with the other Portuguese. The governor expressed surprise at this attitude and questioned our author if the Portuguese were all vassals of the same lord, to which our author replied, they were, being equally liegemen of the king of Portugal, and if Cristovão Jussarte had said that thing, it was because he wished evil to the others.

The next day (*ao outro dya segymte*) our author declares he found the man who Cristovão Jussarte had dispatched by land, who did not speak with the king, as we noted above, and who placed himself in the house of one Martim de Luçena, a Portugal established at the capital of Bengal in circumstances unknown to our history, and this ambassador of Cristovão Jussarte, we are informed, was so racked by fevers that he was near death.

On this same day our author encountered Martim de Luçena, who he failed to recognize since he came dressed as a Moor, and the former greeted our author from a nag (*rocym*), and we are to understand that each knew the other from another occasion.

At a latter day (*ao outro dya*) our author was informed by the governor (*regedor*) that the king desired to see his guests, and thus upon that day Cristovão Jussarte would proceed to court, and at another day (*ao outro dya*) the others. Cristovão Jussarte, we learn, had bribed the governor with three ells of velvet and *gram*-scarlet-in-grain, and some pieces of damask, in order to see the king first, but his efforts availed him little that day, since Cristovão Jussarte was carried to a mosque to await the pleasure of the king of Bengal, and Cristovão Jussarte waited in the mosque until evening without being called, and from the mosque he proceeded to his house without speaking to the king.

"The morning of the next day (*ao outro dya segymte pela menham*), being in the public square to search some things that were necessary, I saw Cristovão Jussarte pass who went to speak to the King and to present his embassy to him.

"I brought the armorer who cleaned the arms [intended for the king] so well, that they could not be better, and we made ourselves ready as directed, and thus we passed that day, and another, and coming the dawn, the governor desired to know if we were ready to speak to the King, as in fact we were, because when he knew we were ready, presently he dispatched fifteen or twenty honored men to go with us to the gates of the palace, where we found that many *fidalgos* and great lords awaited us.

"We saw many people of arms, possessing many flags with diverse emblems, and each had care to guard his own, among which was a great white and blue flag of taffeta with some stars of gold in the midst of the others, which was placed on a very great and long staff that rose above all, and above the flag was a half moon of gold, four spans from point to point and two in height, and above this half moon, a *copa*-crown [or cup?] of gold from which departed a slender rod of gold that possessed a red and white flag likewise of taffeta, and alongside this great flag, three hundred *lasquarys* covered below but nude from the waist above, stood guard, and all these had swords and *adargas*-oval shields and [there were] another so many archers and these shield bearers of whom I speak, had red and white painted shields, and in the middle a lion rampant with black claws, entirely gilded, and in the left paw, a half globe with the claws across it, and in the right [paw], a sword full of blood.

"In front of the first gate of the palaces was a great chain that passes over all the wall from here to a mosque which was on the other side, and it was as thick as a man around the middle, and from this chain, as far as the inside, where there is a great courtyard, neither horse or litter enters save those of great rank.

"Arriving at this gate of which I speak, a *fidalgo* came to us, who was [the] *guarda perena*-perennial guard [?] of the King, to whom the governor, who brought us, delivered us, and after we were delivered, all of us were searched by him, as far as our hair, to see if we carried any arms, and while they searched the others, I looked for something worthy to note, and I saw what I will say below.

"This gate has two vaulted towers, each with four *curucheos*-spires, three in triangle, and a great one in the middle, above which was a sphere of gold as large as a great caldron, and from the inside of it departs a shaft of gold or gold leaf. On the shaft were another so many emblems as those on the great flag of which I have spoken above, which flag I knew belonged to the guard of the King, and from these spheres of which I speak, depart two great horns of gold and on the tip of each [was] a small red and white banner, and thus we were carried to the second door.

"We arrived at the second gate and we were searched as at the first, and we passed by this and by others, as many as nine, and we were searched at each one, and arriving at the last gate, we saw a great courtyard the length of a great track, and half hollow,[*] and so wide, or wider than [it was] long on which twelve men were playing *choqua*-polo on horseback, and at the end of the said courtyard a great dais was set upon thick props of sandalwood, and those above, upon which the roof rested, were not as thick, all carved with *maçanarya*-joinery and [with] many gilded branches and small birds, and the ceiling above in the same manner, and [with] a moon and a sun, with [a] very great number of stars, and all gilded.

"We arrived to where the King was seated on a very great *catere*-divan, likewise gilded, with [a] very large store of great and small pillows, all embroidered, and with many precious stones and seed-pearls on them, and coming before him, we made our reverence to him according to the custom of the land, being with the hands crossed upon the chest and the head bowed as low as possible, and the King, in order to make great honor to us, sat in the right *quama*-receptacle and he smiled at us and then we showed to him the arms which were some cuirasses set in white cordovan

---

* The Portuguese appears to read: *vymos huum tereyRo grande que he de comprydo grande careyRa e mea de cauado*. Possibly, however, I should read *caualo* for *cauado*, in which case the Portuguese translates "we saw a great courtyard the length of a great track, and half for horse[s]".

crauaçõ and gilded collars and a helmet and a *barbote*-armored chin piece and some *espaldaretes*-shoulder pieces and some *coxites*-thigh pieces with all their furnishings gilded and a sword with handles and [a] large mallet with [a] silver grip and [a] *comteyra*-chape of gold with its scabbard in black velvet, and a very good lance with an iron head and an *adarga*-oval shield of tapir.

"After all these things were presented, we showed to him the horse that we carried which was [a] grey Arabian. Mounting it the King rode him, and ordered them to promenade him, and after being well promenaded, the King remained very content with him since he was handsome and well *arremedado*-mimicked. This being concluded, we were taken and carried by certain *fidalgos* who placed us in a chamber beneath this dais and dressed each one of us in a garb of brocade made to the use of the land, and likewise, they gave to each of us *ssua touta* [?] and this worn over our garments and with some *çemgydouros*-encircling bands that encompassed us above the waist, we appeared [as] badly saddled asses, and thus they took us to carry before the King, who, after he saw us in this sad state, commenced to laugh, telling those *fidalgos* that the Portuguese to him appeared dressed to his taste, and I, who was not very content with such mockery, did not wish to consider this, and I looked to see if I could find something of the pomp of the King, and I counted the men of the guard that were in that dais, and I found four hundred men of the guard, all sons of counts and dukes and great lords, the principal men of the land, and all these wore their *traçados*-broad swords trimmed with gold and with silver, with their *cofos*-shields adorned in the same manner, and each one [bore] his *zagumcho*-spear in the hand with its *cotes*-whetstones and sockets of silver, and all their garb [was] of very fine silks and brocade.

"The King asked me if we were very fatigued by our journey, and I responded, although we were greatly fatigued, being in the presence of His Highness was [a] great contentment and reward, which from the part of the King, our lord, we had hoped, and then he ordered us to proceed to our lodgings, and he would give reply to the letters that we carried and dispatch us as soon as possible, and with this we took our leave and went for [the] house, yet a little displeased, [and] I had place to eye my will, and I observed these gates through which we had passed, and I saw that each one was guarded by one hundred and fifty eunuchs, and each one had another so many arms as the guards of which I have spoken above, save one, who had a thick staff of those of Bengal in his hand with two butts of silver, and some red and white *enxarafas*-ornaments of the head, who all the others

obeyed, and having departed from all these gates, they sent
with us men to whom we gave something, since the King
had rewarded us, and thus they went with us to [the] lodgings, and they carried twenty-five cruzados, and still badly
content, and thus they departed, and we were left to repose
[for] forty-five days without the King ever to ask, or to
know, if we were dead or alive, nor to send to provide us
with anything."

During this time a letter arrived from Antonio de Brito at Chatigam
(Chittagong), and our author relates he translated it from Portuguese to their
language (i.e. to Persian) and for a space of five days he attempted to deliver
the letter to the king but was unable to pass the portals of the palace. By
chance one day the secretary (sacretayro) of the king passed his way and
our author asked him to deliver the letter to the king. The secretary replied
this was unnecessary, and in great secrecy related to our author that sentence had
been passed to behead the Portuguese of the entourage of Gonçalo Tavares "and
this by [the] counsel of Magylyz, Rume, who was a dog that was second-captain
of [the] armada of the Rumes that Dom Francisco de Almeida, Viceroy of the
Indies, defeated at Diu," and also by the counsel of Nazyr Quão (Nazir Khan)
"who we called Count Pryall" and Corydo, the stablemaster, who informed the
king that the Portuguese of the embassy of Gonçalo Tavares were spies and that
afterwards they meant to seize the land by force, alleging this had been the
wont of the Portuguese in other lands, and giving in testimony the actions and
words of Cristovão Jussarte, who would not lodge with the party of Gonçalo
Tavares, saying they were some evil villains and their embassy was false, and
that moreover, this Cristovão Jussarte was now dressed as a Moor to the use
of the land with closely-cropped hair and clean-shaven face, and that he had
come to benefit the land and the embassy of Gonçalo Tavares to damage it,
and had said many unseemly things about Diogo Lopes de Sequeira, the governor of India, and Antonio de Brito—and with the actions and words of Cristovão
Jussarte, and of what the three Moors had said to him, the king now resolved
to execute the Portuguese of the conserve of Gonçalo Tavares.

When our author was informed by the secretary of this decision, in the
presence of all who were there, since, as he declares, he was destined to be
beheaded first, since he was the interpreter (lymgoa)—thus our author now
reveals his office to us—he rent his clothes and in a loud voice beseeched the
secretary to carry the letter of Antonio de Brito to the king of Bengal, wherein
His Majesty would find many things of his service, and moreover he entreated
that the king confront him with his accusers, so that he could show His Highness that what they said was false, and that it was not the custom of the Portuguese to seize lands in the manner that his lords had said.

Our author declares that these shouts reached certain parts of the palaces
and that the king was presently informed a certain Portuguese had departed his
senses and that he said things that would greatly please His Majesty, and our
author avers he was carried to the royal presence, and when the King saw the
letter, being informed it was intended for him, he ordered the secretary to
fetch it, and having read it, he directed the same secretary and a Gromalle to
place the lord-accusers and our author (and some other Portuguese) in a

mosque and to take written account of the reasons each side offered upon the matter of the Portuguese spies, and then to show the answers to him as he desired to know the truth.

The Portuguese were placed in the mosque as directed and seated upon some great carpets with which the entire mosque was covered, and our author declares he desired to know his accusers and that he would respond to all and each one by himself.

The lord-accusers spoke in general terms of the alleged misdeeds of the Portuguese, how they conquered Malacca and destroyed the land without reason and had erected a fortress there—and that this had been done by the greatest dog of India (*o pero mayor da Imdea*) i.e. by Afonso de Albuquerque, and that the Portuguese had erected fortresses in other parts and had gained India by deceit.

Our author answered the charges point by point, with many reasons to the contrary, the gist being that the Portuguese had dealt faithfully with their friends, such as the king of Cochin in Malabar, and that the lands of their allies had been ennobled, while the treachery of their enemies had been answered with the condign punishment it merited; Malacca being an instance in point where the treachery perpetrated against Diogo Lopes de Sequeira found retribution in the conquest of Afonso de Albuquerque.

These things having terminated, the Portuguese were carried to the king with the written replies of our author, and when these replies were read to him, he commenced to laugh and questioned our author why, if the Portuguese were such good men, had they seized two of his *naos* in which they misappropriated two hundred and fifty thousand cruzados. Our author responded that the king of Portugal was lord of the sea, and that in those parts where his ships navigated, no others were permitted to sail without his passes. The king apparently swallowed this reply in whole, as we are not informed that he disputed the prerogative of the king of Portugal to the dominion of the Asian seas, although neither the king of Bengal, or any Asian prince, could derive the least contentment from the Portuguese pretensions. At this interview Gromalle, who had gone to Malacca in the lifetime of the king's father, Oçem (Husain, 1493-1519), and during the present reign (i.e. during the kingship of Nusrat Shah, 1519-1532), spoke in favor of the Portuguese, of their justice, and of the honor which he had received from them at Malacca, and stressed their power at sea and the damage which their armadas could inflict upon the commerce of the Kingdom of Bengal, and that it suited the royal service to have the indefatigable Portugals as friends rather than enemies.

After giving a *quabaya*-Turkish tunic to our author, His Majesty of Bengal declared he was pleased to have the friendship of the king of Portugal, and from what follows in the manuscript it appears that Antonio de Brito *o velho* had intended to sail to China in the first instance, but having lost the monsoon, determined instead to sail to Bengal, and that the Portuguese were seeking a reduction of the duties imposed at Bengal, which are described as very high. Being one hour of the night, our author declares he took leave of the king and went to his lodgings. The anonymous author of our manuscript had well conquered Sultan Nusrat Shah and the lords of Bengal!

"After this, fifteen days later, the sun having set, the King sent to call us, and in his presence, Cristovão Jussarte arrived dressed as [a] Moor, and he placed him at one end with those Portuguese who came with him, and being thus, the King asked what things of these parts would please the King of Portugal, and the interpreter of Cristovão Jussarte advanced to speak and responded to him that [the King of Portugal would be pleased] with some bows and some canopies, so that the King, having turned to his great lords, commenced to laugh. Then the secretary beckoned to me. I said ask Your Highness that interpreter and he will tell you the truth since the other [Cristovão Jussarte] has lost control of himself as he shows in his badly concerted words.

"The King then called me with his hand and asked me what things of the land would please the King of Portugal. I responded the King, our lord, has not desired to visit Your Highness save to hope for sincere friendship, and with this intention his governor [of India] dispatched the horse and arms to Your Highness which is a custom among us; firstly we give to those persons whose friendship we desire, because as Your Highness can well see it is not [a] thing for the King, our lord, to send to such a powerful prince as Your Highness; rather it is a sign of friendship, because after the King, our lord, knows how Your Highness is content with his friendship, he will dispatch letters and presents as it suits for two great princes, and with regard to what Your Highness says about the King, our lord, wishing [things] of these lands, you must know the King, our lord, has in Portugal many lands, where each day come *naos* and *navios* loaded with great quantities of gold and silver, and he has many velvets and *gras*-scarlets-in-grain and other cloths of divers manners and great quantities of copper and tin and lead and mercury and cinnabar and [a] very great quantity of coral, which is the merchandise that is greatly valued in these parts."

The Portuguese were called to a large room where they were dressed with *quabayas*-Turkish tunics and *touquas*-turbans and girded after the manner of the first interview, and the king delivered the Portuguese of the entourage of Gonçalo Tavares to a newly appointed governor (*regedor*) of Chittagong, one Mylyque Cuyll, and under penalty of the greatest instance directed him to see that the Portuguese were honorably treated enroute to Chittagong. The king terminated this last interview by declaring his minister (*regedor*) would write to the governor of India (*o voso regedor*).

The Portuguese departed from the capital of Bengal in a *parao* which they purchased, taking leave of Gaur, alas today in ruin, on a Friday, and on the Sunday following they arrived at Noamaluquo.

At Noamaluquo the Portuguese experienced the delays and petty-counterfeits of the governor of the city, and having embarked for Chittagong, two *quystes* accompanied the Portuguese, dispatched by the governor of Noamaluquo with instructions to rob them. Passing near the same places which they had encountered in their ascent of the Ganges, the Portugals were attacked by seven *paraos* of robbers, servants of the governor, as we are informed, who the Portuguese obliged to retire, and since they knew the evil which the two *quystes* intended, they were likewise dismissed.

The Portuguese after their long and hazardous peregrination into the interior of the ancient Kingdom of Bengal, finally arrived at the port of Chittagong on a Wednesday where they were greeted with great shows of pleasure by the company of Antonio de Brito.

✠ ✠ ✠

Before narrating the passage of Antonio de Brito *o velho* to the Kingdom of Pegu in 1522, for we have now reached this point in time, our author offers some notices of Rafael Perestrello, who, as we have seen, passed to Bengal from Pacem in 1521 (Vide Chapter II Section 4). We are informed that Rafael Perestrello had fortified some houses on top of a hill (*outeyro*): he had apparently entered into friendly relations with the Moslems (or at least some of the Moslems of Chittagong). At times the Portuguese of the conserve of Rafael Perestrello, most of whom were dressed to the use of the land, descended from their fortifications and imprisoned the Portuguese of the conserve of Antonio de Brito in the public square of Chittagong "and placed them in irons as though they were Moors." Why this hostility should exist between Rafael Perestrello and Antonio de Brito *o velho*, I do not know, except to note that many, if not most of the Portugals in the Kingdom of Bengal at this time, were not members of the regular establishment, but irregulars, and of a very unsavory variety to the mode of Cristovão Jussarte. With this observation we terminate the account of the voyage of Antonio de Brito to Chittagong, and our description of the embassy of Gonçalo Tavares to the court of Bengal, since the fleet of Antonio de Brito is now preparing to embark for Pegu, and his voyage to Pegu will not be of interest to us in a chapter dedicated to the establishment of Portuguese relations with the ancient Kingdom of Bengal.

BIBLIOGRAPHY

MANUSCRIPTS

1. Anonymous. *Lembrança dalgumas coussas que se passaram quando Amtonio de Bryto e Dyogo Pereyra foram a Bemgalla asy em Bengala como em Tanaçaiym e em Pegu onde tambem fomos.* São Vicente: Vol. 11—Folhas 47-88.

A NOTE WITH REGARD TO THIS MANUSCRIPT

When I went to Lisbon for the second time (i.e. during the winter of 1968-1969) I came upon this manuscript by chance in the Torre do Tombo while looking for a description of the city of Ahmedabad to include in Part II of this volume. I was looking for a description of Ahmedabad, because when I went to Lisbon the first time (i.e. during the winter of 1967-1968) I purchased the *Lendas da India* of Gaspar Correa, and when I brought these volumes home with me, I noticed a reference by Rodrigo José de Lima Felner, who edited this work, to a manuscript entitled *Capitulo das cousas que passarão no Reyno de Guzarate depois da morte de Sultão Modafar* in the collection São Vicente. Unfortunately I never did discover the description of Ahmedabad for which I was looking, but in the same volume of São Vicente, containing the manuscript to which Lima Felner refers, I found the anonymous manuscript of the embassy of Gonçalo Tavares to the court of Bengal. This was a surprise to me because I did not expect to find a work of this length (forty-one folios), and for such an early period of the Portuguese connection with India, and a work of which the sixteenth century Portuguese authors make no reference. Rather I expected to find some letters, for the period 1515-1521 as I found for my *First Age of the Portuguese Embassies, Navigations and Peregrinations to the Kingdoms and Islands of Southeast Asia (1509-1521)*, and with the money I paid to acquire the *História do Descobrimento & Conquista da India pelos Portugueses* by Fernão Lopes de Castanheda, a native of the ancient city of Santarem, whose mountain I have climbed, and with the money I wanted to pay to have this manuscript, and some other documents transcribed for me, I remained in such need that I was obliged to write my parents for help.

After I had a chance to read some parts of this manuscript—some parts because the sixteenth century script is very difficult for me to read, and as a rule, I can read the script only for names and dates, and for some other things—after reading the manuscript I went to Padre Antonio da Silva Rego, some of whose works I have read with great attention, principally his *As Gavetas da Torre do Tombo*, and I asked if he knew if this manuscript had been published, and he said no, and I asked him if he could arrange to have this manuscript transcribed for me in its entirety, and he obliged me by directing one of his people, Senhorita Maria Luisa Meireles Pinto, to copy this document for me, and it is from her transcription that I have gathered my intelligence for the embassy of Gonçalo Tavares.

The manuscript is part of a sixteenth century codice containing sundry notices of the Portugals in Asia, principally of a later period than that covered by our manuscript, which, according to Padre Schurhammer, who has seen this manuscript, is a copy of the time (*abschrift der zeit*), and this appears to be just since this manuscript is in the same hand as some other manuscripts and notices of the same codice. Padre Schurhammer gives a brief notice of this manuscript in his catalogue: *

> "[A] participant describes [the] journey of the embassy of
> Antonio de Brito o Velho to [the] King of Bengal at Gauel
> [Gaur] and [the] King of Pegu. Description of Gaur: 914
> war-elephants, 4500 horses: [the] king has 2500 women and
> 3000 from his father. *Sehr wertvoller Bericht.*"

Sehr wertvoller Bericht or a very valuable account; each will judge it according to his interest. It is certainly a valuable account of the embassy of Gonçalo Tavares and contains a splendid description of Gaur (See Chapter XX). This note, and another of Padre Schurhammer, which I saw in a Portuguese journal,

---

* *Die Zeitgenössischen Quellen zur Geschichte Portugiesisch-Asiens und seiner Nachbarländer zur Zeit des Hl. Franz Xaver (1538-1552)*, Rome, 1962.

I can not remember where, are the only notices I have encountered of the embassy of Gonçalo Tavares.

The Portuguese of this manuscript is very archaic and reduced to the clear hand of my copyist, it is still very difficult to read. Words to complete the meaning of the author's thoughts are often wanting, while other words have been inadvertently repeated, and the same term is often spelled in two, or even three different ways. For my part I have inserted the words to clarify the meaning of quotations in square brackets. However I have not included (in the same quotations) the inadvertent repetitions, judging these to be the errors of the scribe of the manuscript, that do not pertain to the anonymous author of the same, and hence are unnecessary to repeat.

ARAKAN

CHAPTER III

THE VOYAGE OF DOM JOAM DA SILVEIRA—1518

Recall that Dom João da Silveira received an invitation to visit Arakan. We departed Dom João at Chittagong, to conclude our study of the establishment of Portuguese relations with the Kingdom of Bengal, and having brought that enterprise to a conclusion, it remains for us to terminate the voyage of Dom João da Silveira with an inquiry into what transpired with his affairs in the Kingdom of Arakan, and thus in consideration of our promise in Chapter II Section 2 to follow his armada to Arakan.

Dom João da Silveira, João Fidalgo, Tristão Barbudo, João Moreno, Gaspar Fernandes, and the mariners of their valiant conserve, sailed to the mouth of the rio Arracam* in the company of the Arakanese ambassador and the members of his retinue. Here the Portuguese discovered numerous *calaluzes* and *lancharas* awaiting their arrival with produce and refreshment in great abundance. The Arakanese received the fleet with great celebration.

Dom João da Silveira—destination the Cidade Arracam,** fifteen leagues from the mouth of the river—ascended the rio Arracam with his fleet expecting to secure the blessings of friendship and peace from the king of Arakan, Minyaza (1501-1523), and to provision the fleet with the equipment which he sought. Castanheda notes Dom João sought to found a factory at the city of Arakan.

Ten leagues from the entrance of the rio Arracam, Dom João passed a stockade that appeared to him a work innocent of evil employment. Passing ahead, the river narrowed, and the flagship could scarcely fit, and the *antenas da verga*-yard-spars grazed the branches of the trees of a tropical rain forest. On the one side, as upon the other, the luxuriant jungle of Arakan overspread the river in a leafy embrace.

"... in these surroundings [Dom João da Silveira] dispatched the Ambassador, declaring he could well perceive how his vessel could not navigate on such [a] narrow thing; if the King desired to see him, it would have to be at that place, where they could settle peace, and friendship, and for this he would wait for two days until he saw his message. The ambassador when he perceived the force of reason against him, [and] that he could not induce him to go forward indicated he would not linger the two days, since the City [of Arakan] was at hand. He departed, carrying with him the craft of his company, but he did not return in three, nor four [days]. In this time—since D. João kept vigil on the river with two *bargantijs*—above, and below,—one of

* "Arracão, rio de—The river Kaladan, we suppose, whose waters discharge into the Bay of Bengal in 20° 09′ lat. N. and 92° 57′ long. E. at the [town of] Akyab." (Visconde de Lagoa)

** "Arracão, cidade de—The City of Myo-Haung or Arakan of the English maps in 20° 36′ lat. N. and 93° 15′ long E. in Burma." (Visconde de Lagoa)

them came to him to say that at a certain narrow pass, through which they had passed below, where they found the beginnings of a stockade, there were many people adding posts as though they intended to cross the river. D. João in passing upstream had seen the commencement of this stockade, and it appeared to him to be [a] device of the fishermen, as they use in those parts. However when he knew there were many people at work upon it, he understood his mistake, and as another disaster such as that which happened to D. Lourenço de Almeida in the river of Chaul, might happen to him, without further delay he started downstream. When he passed the said stockade, the people of the work fled, as though they feared they would receive some injury from our people, for they understood the betrayal which they sought to effect." (Barros, Decada III Livro II Capitulo III)

Dom João da Silveira reached the mouth of the rio Arracam in safety, notwithstanding the enmity of his enemies, and having tasted the hostility of the king of Arakan, and having awaited for some message from the royal behalf, without receiving one, Dom João did not wish to remain longer in the parts of Bengal and Arakan, and set sail for the island of Ceylon where Lopo Soares de Albergaria, his uncle, had promised him the captaincy of the fortress on that island. Arriving at Ceylon in the end of November of 1518, Dom João received the captaincy of the fortress of Colombo from the hands of the governor, who in this same year had sailed to Ceylon with the purpose of erecting a fortress, and who had just (or nearly) completed it when Dom João arrived from Arakan.

"And [Dom João da Silveira and his fleet], having departed [for Ceylon], João Fidalgo rebelled against his command and returned to the mouth of this rio Darracão [river of Arakan] to make prizes of the *naos* that he knew would depart from it, and to dissemble, he dispatched a present to the lord [i.e. the king] of Arakan by two of our people, relating by means of them that the captain-major had left him there to settle peace with him, in as much as he could not await his coming, as it was late, and he had great occupations in other parts. And the lord of Arakan seeing both our people who carried this message to him, with the present, immediately ordered their deaths, and as he could not be avenged against the captain-major, he would find his revenge in João Fidalgo, dispatching many *lancharas* and *calaluzes*, with people of war to capture him, and they would have done so if Our Lord had not freed him miraculously. He fought with the enemy for nearly a day, in which they nearly entered, and they injured forty of his [João Fidalgo's] people, and he had no remedy other than to cut his anchor cables by which he was anchored, and with the wind that blew he found safety, without the enemy being able to reach him, and from that place he sailed

99

and wandered to many different parts where some of his men were killed and others were captured[*] without taking any prizes, and at last he returned to India where the Governor Diogo Lopes de Sequeira pardoned him." (Castanheda, Livro IV Capitolo XXXIX)

---

* It is curious to note that in the anonymous manuscript from which we narrated the embassy of Gonçalo Tavares to the court of Bengal (Chapter II Section 6), the author, referring to the year 1522, in a brief statement, notes there were Portuguese captives in Arakan (*Araguão*), without noting the place (or places) of their incarceration, or their numbers, or the circumstances and date of their captivity.

Barros, Decada III Livro II Capitulo III
Castanheda, Livro IV Capitolo XXXIX
Goes, Parte IV Capitulo XXVII
We have noted from the part of Antonio de Miranda de Azevedo (Chapter II Section 3) that Dom Francisco de Travamqua rebelled against the command of Dom João da Silveira coming the latter from the coast of Bengal and Arakan. Damião de Goes avers other *naos* fled for João Fidalgo, when he revolted, and with him, scoured the Bay of Bengal for prizes. However João de Barros and Fernão Lopes de Castanheda indicate, by their silence, João Fidalgo alone of the original squadron revolted, and they are preferred since they have consulted the primary sources, no longer extant, while Goes for the *ultramar* is generally a copyist, and usually of Castanheda, from whom he has chosen to differ in the present instance.

BIBLIOGRAPHY

PRINTED SOURCES

1. Barros, João de. *Da Asia*, Vol. 5, Lisbon, 1777.
2. Castanheda, Fernão Lopes de. *História do Descobrimento & Conquista da India pelos Portugueses*, Coimbra, Imprensa da Universidade, 1928.
3. Goes, Damião de. *Crónica do Felicissimo Rei D. Manuel*, Coimbra, Imprensa da Universidade, 1926.

DOCUMENTS

1. Letter of Dom João de Lima to the King D. Manuel—Cochin, December 22, 1518. Corpo Cronológico: Parte I Maço 23 Documento 117.

MANUSCRIPTS

1. Anonymous. *Lembrança dalgumas coussas que se passaram quando Amtonio de Bryto e Dyogo Pereyra foram a Bemgalla asy em Bengala como em Tanaçaiym e em Pegu onde tambem fomos.* São Vicente: Vol. 11—Folha 80.

✠ ✠ ✠

EXTRACT OF THE LETTER OF DOM JOAM DE LIMA TO KING MANUEL
DESCRIBING THE VOYAGE OF DOM JOAM DA SILVEIRA TO
THE KINGDOMS OF BENGAL AND ARAKAN
Dated Cochin, 22nd December 1518

"Dom João [da Silveira], lord, was in Bengal this past winter and there he wintered. He was always at war until the end and did not make any contraction of peace with them. They say the people are very weak and perverse. They concealed all the things of the land from him. They say silver, and coral, and copper are of great value there, yet none of these things did they wish to purchase, and the reason for this, lord, was because of some Guzerate *naos* that were there, which caused all this difficulty.

"The land is very bountiful. Ten bundles of rice are worth one *pardao*, that is three hundred and twenty *reis*, with each bundle at three *alqueires*, and this is the *giracall* rice, and twenty chickens for a *tanga*, which is three *vintens*, and another so many at ten, and three *varas* to the *pardao*, and the money of this land is *buzios* [cowries] because no one save the King of the land, is allowed to have gold and silver.

"The people are dusky and the speech is nearly that of Goa. This [land] lies upon the shores of the Bay of Bengal, opposite this of India, and is in twenty degrees of the part of the north, which is the latitude of Diu, and a male slave is worth six *tangas* and a youthful Gentile woman another so many.

"At the bar of this River [of Chittagong], lord, there are three good fathoms at low tide. The water rises from three to six at high tide. They say it is two small leagues from the bar to the city [of Chittagong]. The city is very large, and with many people, and very weak. Dom João remained here for five months [from May until October] awaiting the monsoon to come to India, and having departed from Bengal, they [Dom João and company] arrived at the mouth of a river where they entered for three leagues. The place to which this river passes is called Raquam [Arakan] and the King has war with Bengal. This King, whilst Dom João was in Bengal, sent two *paraos* to him with provisions, [informing him] that he desired to be [a] friend and vassal of Your Highness, and that they should proceed to his port and that there they would find many commodities: ivory, and *lacre*-lac and wearing-apparel and precious stones, and if Dom João so desired, he would go with his people to assist him make war against Bengal. From that place [of Arakan] Dom João departed without to speak to the King, nor to see the city [of Arakan (Myo-Haung)], because it was from where they emerged, two leagues to the place, and there he was provided with *paraos*, if he should have need of water or firewood, which they gave to him, and from here they departed for the return to Ceylon where they found Lopo Soares making the fortress, from whom Dom João had the captaincy, as I have said to Your Highness."

Corpo Cronológico: Parte I Maço 23
Documento 117 of the Torre do
Tombo

101

PART II

DESCRIPTIONS

CHAPTER IV

DESCRIPTION OF THE KINGDOM OF DIUL (i.e. SIND) BY DUARTE BARBOSA

The Kingdom of Diul is an independent nation. It marches with the great Kingdom of Cambay, on the one side, and with the land of Persia on the other side. The king is obedient to Xeque Ismael (Sheikh Ismael; also Ismael Shah—the king of Persia, 1502-1524). The king of Diul is a Moor, and likewise a great lord of many people and lands in the interior. He possesses numerous horses but has very few ports on the sea. Most of the people are Moors and some are Gentiles. The Gentiles are greatly subject to the Moors of the kingdom. The Moors of Diul are white men, and men of dusky complexions, and speak their own language. They also speak Persian and Arabic.

Diul is a flat land; a land of open country with very little wood. Wheat and barley are cultivated. It has meats in great abundance. The land is fruitful, flourishing and provided with many provisions.

The people of Diul are not wont to sail abroad. Yet as the land possesses noble and numerous beaches, they construct a great number of beautiful fisheries, and they catch very large fish of all kinds, which are dried, and then freighted for shipment to the interior, and thus for many other parts. In this kingdom they feed their horses with dried fish. Some of the *naos* which come to the Kingdom of Diul from India (i.e. from the other parts of India) carry large quantities of rice, sugar, some spices, wood, *tauoado*-planks and some Indian canes, or reeds, as thick as the leg of a man. The merchants gain a good deal of money for these things. In return they freight with large quantities of cotton, cloths and horses.

From this Kingdom of Diul a great river comes from the middle of Persia and discharges into the sea (alas Barbosa is speaking of the Indus whose sources are discovered among the mountains of the Hindu Kush and the Himalayas and not in the midst of Persia). Upon this river there are many rich places belonging to the Moors.

Livro de Duarte Barbosa

CHAPTER V

DESCRIPTION OF THE KINGDOM OF CAMBAY BY DUARTE BARBOSA

The king of Cambay is a great lord—a Moor who holds splendid court. He is called Sultan Moordafaa (Muzaffar II, 1511-1526). His father was Sultan Mahamude (Mahmud I, 1458-1511). His men-at-arms are Moors. His kingdom is opulent and populous. Sultan Moordafaa possesses four to five hundred elephants that come from Ceylon and Malabar. They are sold at his ports. His elephants are large and handsome creatures. The king pays fifteen hundred cruzados (more or less) for each elephant that he buys. With his elephants and horses, Sultan Moordafaa wages great wars against the Rajputs

(*Resbutos*) and thus against sundry other kings as occasion and circumstance dictate.

When the elephants proceed to war they carry a castle of wood upon their backs with three or four men carrying muskets, bows and arrows, and divers arms to engage the enemy. The elephants are well-instructed in the art of war, and attack the enemy (both horse and men) with their powerful tusks. However, if they are injured, they are apt to rout their own forces.

The Moors of Cambay are excellent horsemen. They ride with high-pommelled saddles (*caualgaom ha bastarda*). In war they bear circular shields that are very strong, and garnished with silk. Each Moor carries two swords, a dagger, and a Turkish bow with a store of fine arrows. Other horsemen carry maces of steel, and others wear coats of mail and yet others wear *laudeês*-buff coats quilted with cotton. Their horses are covered with front pieces of steel. These Moors have broad swords finely damascened with gold and silver, and this, according to the rank of the man. These broad swords are borne by their pages. These people fight well. The Moorish horsemen play the game of *choqua*-polo in the saddle, which they esteem as the Portuguese do the game of reeds, and this is a game well suited to their dexterity on horseback.

The Moors of Cambay are white men and the majority of them are foreigners from sundry parts; they are Turks, Mamelukes, Arabians, Persians, Khurasanis, Turcomans, men of the Kingdom of Delhi, and still others are natives of Cambay. The foreigners gather in Cambay because the land is a great emporium, to which ships come in plenty, and since the land is rich, the soldiers of Cambay receive good pay for their services.

The Moors of Cambay are men well dressed, wearing cloths of gold, silk, cotton and camlet. They wear *touquas*-turbans upon their heads. Their dress is long, similar to the Moorish shirts (i.e. the jibbas of the Arabs), with draws, and *brozeguis*-boots extending to the knees made of very fine cordovan leather, cut very subtly in leather strips, inside and out with fine edging.

The Moorish women are white and lovely. They are well attired. When a Moorish woman leaves her house, she is conveyed in a horse drawn carriage, in all respects well covered, so that no one may see who rides inside. The Moors are very jealous of their women. A marriage may be terminated by either party. The husband, however, must pay his wife a sum of money which he promised her at the time of their marriage, and this, in view of the contingency of divorce. A Moorish man, in honor of the Mohammedan sect, may marry as many women as he can support. Some men have four and five wives. Their wives have pretty hair.

The Moors of Cambay are luxuriant men, given to the good things of life. They are great spenders. They wear their hair closely cropped. They speak a variety of languages, including Turkish, Arabic and Guzerate. They eat bread of wheat, rice and excellent meats of all kinds save what is forbidden by their law.

The old King Mahamude (Mahmud I) was raised on poison, taking small quantities at first to increase his resistance to its harmful effects, and thus to remain immune from death by that agency should fate declare him a victim of some plot, or other, which the Moors are wont to raise against their kings.

Livro de Duarte Barbosa

103

CHAPTER VI

DESCRIPTION OF THE KINGDOM OF CAMBAY, THE GULF OF CAMBAY, RAJASTHAN AND OF SUNDRY RELATED TOPICS BY JOAM DE BARROS

"The things of India, and of the other Oriental Provinces, which the Portuguese have discovered and conquered, being so novel, and unknown to the men of Europe, and so worthy to be brought to the attention of the World, and of which the ancient Greeks and Romans have left so little written: the Romans since their Empire did not reach those parts, and the Greeks since their dominion did not endure very long in some of the parts which they once possessed; it should not appear foreign to the matter that we purpose, namely to write about the deeds which the Portuguese have made in those parts, to relate something of the situation of the lands, of the origin of their people, and of their Kings, and Princes, of their customs and sects, and of the mode of their soldiery, for thus we shall better understand this History, and be able to gather the respect with which we ought to esteem the Portuguese, who so many, and such ferocious nations, so many times conquered and brought beneath their yoke; and receiving from them homage and tribute, as conquerors and their lords, gave to them laws, language and to many Religion.

"Since our things are so closely joined to these people, thus in war, as for the commerce that we have with them, we shall not be able to write of our things without likewise touching upon theirs. And besides the necessity which we have of treating part of their things in order to better understand ours, it is no little ornament, and utility for history, by way of example, and admonition of our life, to relate varieties of enterprises, and [the] ends for which they were intended, and their results, for with their notice we shall arrive at judgement and prudence, for we shall be able to govern ourselves in similar things, which is the principal end and fruit of history. . . .

"The Kingdom of Guzarate, which we generally call *Cambaya* [Cambay in English] . . . commences at the point of Jaquete [Jakad, at the western tip of Kathiawar], and terminates in the Nagotana River, which is the limit of the said Kingdom, and by the lands of Chaul, which belong to the Seigniory of Nizamaluco [Nizam-ul-Mulk]. And to better comprehend the situation of this Kingdom, we shall employ our left hand. . . . With this hand turned palms down, the fingers joined, and separating the thumb from the rest, we have the Gulf of Cambay; and in the part where it curves

104

the most, at the juncture of the thumb, upon the side of [the] inside, is situated the City of Cambayet, which we call *Cambaya*, which, since it is the most noble and populous, being the Metropolis of those maritime places, gives its name not only to the same gulf but to the entire Kingdom. However the nobility and trade which it formerly possessed, as it was celebrated, it lost when the City of Diu was founded as we shall declare ahead, because the navigation from that City is so dangerous by reason of the great bore which it possesses, that when the tide fills and empties, many *naos* are overturned. This bore, or flood of the tide, is so swift that there is no horse, however nimble, which the tide does not overtake when it enters by the *planicie*-floor of the gulf, so that a great deal of property and many people are lost in the Carcarij [Mahi] River, which flows into the last recess of this gulf, above the said City of Cambay. In the mouth of this river, so as to prevent the loss of people, by order of those who rule the land, there is always a lookout in a high place, who perceiving the coming of the tide from afar, which invariably comes so high and proud, that it appears to be a mountain of water, and as it commences to make its appearance, that lookout blows a horn in order to give notice that no one should pass the river; because the tide comes with such precipitation and such fury, and pours such a great quantity of water into that passage, that it overwhelms all. And if this lookout failed to descry the tide, there is another very certain sign of its onrush; that is the great number of birds which come to that tidal estuary in search of the refuse of the sea, which by natural instinct, even though they do not perceive the tide, when its onset is imminent such is the cackling and whistling they make fleeing for land, that they are heard from great distances even if unseen. And by reason of this very dangerous bore there is an arm of the sea in the City of Cambay where the *navios* gather, removing themselves from the violence of the tide that runs straight to fetch the narrows of the river where it makes the damage that we have mentioned.

"The City of Diu does not have this danger, rather its navigation is very advantageous since that City is situated upon the point of the thumb, which we use for a figure, that remains against the West, and whence run all the *naos* that go from both straits, of Ormuz and of Mecca, and thus of all the coast of Melinde, which, when they wish to pass to India, that is the entire part of the fore-finger which runs from the second joint as far as the terminal point, this City of Diu remains virtually as an entrepot for the East and for the West, since this Kingdom has a greater supply of merchandise, imported and exported, than in all of India, excluding pepper and other spices that originate in the land of Malabar towards the East.

"And returning to our division of this Kingdom of Guzarate, from the knuckle in the middle of the fore-finger, which we figure to be the Nogatana River, [the] Eastern term of this Kingdom, as far the City of Diu, this coast with its curves after its manner, has eighty leagues and running as far as the point of Jaquete [Jakad or Dwarka] one hundred and twenty-five. By [the] inside, in the interior of the part of the West, which is the thumb, it marches with the *póvos Resbutos* [i.e. with the Rajputs]. These people inhabit a cord of mountain ranges and forest, which begin near Cape Jaquete and run towards the North and Northeast as far as the Kingdom [of] Mandou [Malwa], which rests upon the juncture of this thumb, so that the Kingdom of Guzarate also marches with this Kingdom on the part of the North, and upon the Northeast with the Kingdom of Chitor, and in the East with that of Pale [Khandesh], comprehending all the coast of the Gulf that we have mentioned, where there are numerous Cities and villages.

"Almost all of the maritime portions of this Kingdom, principally those of the side of the East, in addition to being flat land, are watered by two notable rivers: [the] Taptij [Tapti] and Tapetij [Narmada], and they have many inlets of salt water, which cut into the shore to form Islands. This part is very fecund with provisions of all kinds and with great abundance of livestock which graze upon their fertile meadows. And it is the same on the other side of the coast of the West, although it lacks that abundance of waters; and upon the sea-littoral the land rises and lowers some what, so that this portion remains mountainous with respect to the other side.

"Departing from the sea-littoral and proceeding for the Mountains of the Resbutos [Rajputs] on the part of the West, and of the North and Northeast, where this Kingdom separates from the Kingdoms that we noted, virtually all [the land] is open country, so flat, that all the service of the people is in carriages conveyed by oxen, which do not proceed so heavily as ours of Hispania, nor are so large, but [the oxen] are much more lively in their gait than Moorish donkeys, and they have in their stride more *assento*-ease than the *facas*-hackney horses of Ireland, in such a manner, according to what some of our people say, who have tested these two modes of conveyance, those who proceed in these carriages of Cambay, experience less work than those who ride in horse-drawn carriages of Italy and Flanders, and they have [a] better trip, principally in short journeys.

"This entire Kingdom of Guzarate is very well peopled by four kinds of people, of natives of the same land, called Baneanes, of two varieties: some are Bagançarijs, who eat flesh and fish; and some [are] Baneanes [Jains] who do not eat anything that possesses [animate] life; others are Resbutos [Rajputs], who in ancient times were the noblemen of that land, [who are] also Gentiles; others [are] Moors called Luteas, who are natives of the land, newly converted to the sect of Mohammed; others are Moors who came from foreign parts and conquered the land, and expelled the Resbutos. The common people are very industrious, thus in the things of agriculture, as for the mechanical arts, and in this part they are so subtle and enterprising that they have, with the trade in the articles which they manufacture, enriched that Kingdom, because more silk and *ouro fiado*-gold thread is expended in woven cloths of diverse sorts, than in all of India; and in number of looms the City of Patam [Pattan] is able to compete with the Cities of Florence and Milan. Of ivory, of mother-of-pearl, turtle shells, *laquequa*-carnelian, crystal, *lacre*-lacquer, varnish, black and yellow wood, and other things that serve for *leitos*-bedsteads, chairs, vases, and arms of all sorts, from this Kingdom alone more works are exported than from all the rest of India. And henceforth it comes to be supplied with all necessary things; because those things which they do not possess, naturally or artificially, are brought to them by those who come to fetch what they have, and these [commodities] are numerous.

"The common people are naturally weak, and of a servile condition, since they are of the Baneane lineage, who guard with great respect the sect of Pythagoras; not to eat anything that lives. And they are so superstitious in the observance of this precept—that one should not kill, that the vermin which nurture upon one's person, they shake off, in part, so as to avoid injury to them. For which when the Moors wish to take advantage of them, they bring a bird in front of them, or any other animal, even if it is a snake, and acting as if they wished to kill it, these people buy it, and they release it so as not to be a witness to its death, and by this [act] they hold they make [a] great service to God. Even if a track of ants should cross by a way upon which some Baneane goes, either on foot, or on horseback, he is obliged to proceed around so as not to pass over them. By precept of their religion they are not allowed to have any arms in [their] houses; and they are a people more adept and shrewd in the transactions of commerce, than any other people we have discovered, save the Chinese, who in this and in the mechanical arts, carry [the] advantage to all the nations of the world. The other people of this Kingdom, now converted to the sect of

107

the Moors, inasmuch as they are likewise weak, as they are
[a] mixture of both these races, for the part which they have
from the Moors, who are foreigners, they give birth to a more
robust people, [and] make to these Gentiles much advantage.
And of all these people, the most valiant men in war are the
Resbutos [Rajputs] who inhabit the mountain ranges that
we have mentioned, who formerly were lords of this Kingdom of Guzarate, and with the coming of the Moors they
gathered in the highest parts as the Spanish did when the
Moors entered Hispania, withdrawing to the Pyrenees and to
the mountains of Oviedo. And since that time there has
always been a capital hate between the Resbutos and the
others, and they fought with each other. And as the Resbutos
were from the most noble people, who dominated that land
of Guzarate, and are great and forceful men, and do not have
the religion of the Baneanes; armed, and on good horses, they
descend from the mountains and come to the villages below
where they make great prizes. The Resbutos govern themselves at present in Republics by the [counsel of the] eldest,
divided into Lordships; and if all would conform in friendship, and not contend amongst themselves, they would now
be lords of Guzarate which their grandfathers had lost. However with this division, and with the power of artillery, which
they lack, since they do not have commerce by sea, their
valor and spirit do not profit them for more than these
entrances which we have made mention. And what principally made these Moorish Kings, who conquered that Kingdom, powerful against this robust and warlike people, was
that presently they made themselves lords of the seaports,
because to these went many people [of] Arabia, Persia and
Turkey, Greeks by race and of the Levant, which are called
Rumes, who each year come to that Kingdom to fetch merchandise and to gain great wages as soldiers which these
Moorish Kings give to them, with whom they have conquered what they now possess, and defended it from us after
we conquered India. Our entrance was [the] cause of these
Resbutos to lose all of the flat lands which they once possessed; because as the Moorish Kings, defending themselves
from our Armadas, had great need to collect those foreign
people that we mentioned, it gave to them truly the industry
and spirit to defend themselves from the Resbutos, in whose
religion and belief in three Persons, and only one God, and
veneration of the Virgin Mary, Our Lady, and other things, it
appears they have their chief tenets from the Apostles, [and]
in our Geography [a lost work of Barros] we write particularly of it."

Da Asia, Decada IV Livro V Capitulo I

CHAPTER VII

DESCRIPTION OF THE TIDAL FLOOD IN THE GULF OF CAMBAY FROM THE PEN OF DIOGO DE COUTO

"The flux and reflux of the tide in the depths of this Gulf [of Cambay] is so proud and impetuous that you lose sight of it; and if it chances to strike a *navio*, in [the] part that it touches, it is broken in pieces in an instant. And whosoever is in the City of Cambayete [Cambay], beginning the tide to ebb, in a brief space he perceives all empty and dry, as far as the vision carries, save a little canal where the *navios* are supported for both parts with girders that they have for this; and afterwards, when the tide commences to flow, it comes with such pride, making a tidal bore so terrifying, that it appears to desire to engulf the entire City; and it brings with it such a trembling of the earth, that, being I in the City, the first night that we heard it, we were greatly frightened by it, because it appeared that the City was about to be consumed, and in [a] very short period of time all became a sea of water, so that there appeared to be nothing that could dry it.

"And wishing I for curiosity to test this bore, I placed myself upon the seashore on a very swift Arabian horse (in [the] part where only the small breaker of the billow could come). And in perceiving the bore come with great trembling of the earth [at] a great distance, I spurred the horse forward; but rather than a shot of stone, it passed me like a bolt of lightning, leaving me well soaked. And whosoever takes care to note Pliny [alas Ptolemy, *Geography*, Book VII] and Arrian, [a] Greek Author [the anonymous *Periplus of the Erythraean Sea*, sometimes falsely attributed to Arrian] speaking of the City of Bagariza (that without doubt is this of Cambayete, as in another place we will show), will see that clearly they speak of this bore, because they say that the City of Bagariza is in seventeen degrees, and that it has a great river, and whirlpool, and thrust of waters."

Da Asia, Decada VI Livro IV Capitulo III

CHAPTER VIII

DESCRIPTION OF THE RAJPUTS, JAINS AND BRAHMANS OF THE KINGDOM OF CAMBAY BY DUARTE BARBOSA

"Formerly the Kingdom [of Cambay] belonged to [the] Gentiles, and the Moors took it by war; hence the King is now [a] Moor although there are still many Gentiles, [who are] great merchants, and these have dealings amongst each other. Before the Kingdom of Guzarate [i.e. Cambay] pertained to the Moors, it had some Gentiles who the Moors call Resbutos [Rajputs] who in former times were the cavaliers and defenders of the land and made war where neces-

109

sary. These [Rajputs] kill, and eat meat and fish, and all kinds of viands, and even now there are many who live in the mountains where they possess very great places, and do not obey the King of Cambay; rather each day they make great war to him, who, with all his power, is not strong enough to destroy them, nor could he, since they are very good cavaliers and excellent bowmen, and they have many other manners of arms by which they defend themselves very well from the Moors, with whom they are continually at war, without having either King or Lord to govern them.[*]

"The Kingdom [of Cambay] has another kind of Gentile which they call Bramanes,[**] and they are very great merchants and swindlers. They live among the Moors with whom they do all their trading. These people eat neither meat or fish, nor anything that lives [i.e. is any form of sentient life]; neither do they kill, nor less wish to be witness to a killing, for thus they preserve their idolatry; and they guard against this to such a degree that it is a surprising thing, because on many occasions the Moors carry live insects and birds to them, and they act as though they desire to kill these creatures, in their presence, and these Bramanes [alas Baneanes] purchase and redeem them, giving for these much more than what they are worth, so as to save their lives and to free them. Likewise if the King or the governor of the land has some man, sentenced to death for his crimes, they join together and purchase the justice, if it is for sale, in order to prevent a death; and moreover some Moorish beggars, when they desire alms of them, take very large stones and hit themselves upon the shoulders and belly, as if they meant to kill themselves, in their presence, and so they will not do it, they give them many alms, and then they go in peace. Others bring knives, and slash themselves upon the arms and legs, and so they will not kill themselves they render many alms. Others come to their doors wishing to behead rats and snakes, to whom they give great sums of money so they will not do it, and in this manner these people are well appreciated by the Moors.

* Ala-ud-din, sultan of Delhi, dispatched Ulugh Khan and Nusrat Khan to attack Gujarat in 1299. The Turks plundered the kingdom but returned to Delhi in the same year. In 1304-1305, under Malik Ahmed and Panjuman, they came to stay, and from this date commences the Moslem occupation of the Kingdom of Cambay; See the *Tarikh-i-Firuz Shahi* by Zia-ud-din Barni and *The Rise of Muslim Power in Gujarat* by S. C. Misra.

** *Bramanes* is the Portuguese for Brahman. However the Portuguese text is corrupt, and it should read *Baneanes*, i.e. Banians in our English, as is evident from the full text and from what will follow. Barbosa now proceeds to describe the Jain religion with great vividness and accuracy.

"These Bramanes [Baneanes], if they discover a track of ants along the way, they will step aside to search for a place to pass without treading upon them; and in their houses they sup by day; [neither] by day or by night do they light [an] oil lamp, because some of the *mosquitos* [lit. mosquitoes, but in the sense of flying bugs in the present instance] would die in the flame of the lamp. Nevertheless if they have great need to have light at night, they have a lantern with paper or with *pano agomado*-varnished cloth, so that nothing shall lose its life in the flame. If these [Baneanes] give birth to many lice, they do not kill them, and when these become unbearable they fetch some men who live amongst them, who are likewise Gentiles, and who they consider to lead holy lives, and they are similar to *irmytães*-hermits, living in great self-denial for reverence of their Gods; they pluck these, and as many lice as they remove they put on their heads, and nurture them on their flesh, saying they do [a] very great service to their Idol, and thus some observe, and others with more moderation, the law of not to kill, and for another part they are very great usurers and falsifiers of weights and measures, and of many other wares and moneys, and very great liars.

"These Gentiles are dusky men, very well formed; refined men, and gallant in their dress, very dainty and temperate in their eating habits. Their diet consists of milk, butter, sugar, rice and many conserves in divers manners. They consume many fruits, vegetables and greens of [the] field for their nutriment. Wherever they live, they have many gardens and orchards, and many reservoirs of water in which they bathe twice daily, thus men as well as women; and they declare as they finish bathing themselves, that they are saved from so many sins which they have at that hour.

"These Bramanes [Baneanes] let their hair grow very long after the manner of women in our parts, and they wear it gathered upon the head, and fashion it into a *trunfa*-knot, and on top a *touqua*-turban, since they always wear their hair gathered, and with flowers and other fragrant things in it. They are much accustomed to anoint themselves with white sandalwood mixed with *asafram*-saffron and other sweet-smelling things. These men are very amorous. They wear long shirts of cotton and of silk. They wear very well cut shoes with edging of cordovan leather. They wear some short tunics of silk cloth or brocade and they do not bear any arms, only some very small knives worked in gold and silver; this for two reasons, first because they are men to whom arms are of little service and secondly, because the Moors protect them. They use many ear-rings of gold and many precious stones, and rings upon the fingers, and sashes

111

of gold upon their cloths. The wives of these Gentiles are very beautiful, very delicate and with very good figures. They are light brown [in complexion], almost white. Their attire is in silk, as long as that of their husbands. They wear some *sainhos* of silk cloth with close-fitting sleeves, exposed at the back, and other noble cloths which they call *chandes-chadars* that they raise above themselves after the manner of mantles, when they go outside. On the head they do not place a thing, save their hair very well gathered upon it. They always go barefoot. They wear very great rings of gold and silver on their legs, and on the toes and hands [they wear] many rings, and the ears are pierced with great openings through which an egg is able to fit, whence they wear very great ear-rings of gold or silver. [The] women are very shy and withdrawn. They seldom depart from their houses, and when they leave home they are well covered with those great cloths upon the head as the women in our parts cover themselves with their mantles.

"In these parts there is another kind of Gentile who they call Bramenes [Brahmans] who are their priests and [the] persons who administer and govern their houses of prayer and idolatries which possess great revenues and are very large. Also many of these are maintained with alms, in which there are great numbers of wooden idols, others of stone, and copper; in the said houses or monasteries they perform great ceremonies with many plays of the instrument, and many songs, with many lamps and lamps of oil, and with bells after our manner. These Bramenes [Brahmans] and Gentiles have a great deal [in their faith] resembling the Holy Trinity. They greatly honor the notion of three [persons] in one god, and they always make their prayer to God, who they acknowledge and worship as the true God, creator and maker of all things, who is three Persons in only one God, and who has many other Gods, governors for him, in whom they also believe. These Bramenes [Brahmans] and Gentiles wherever they are found, enter our churches and make prayer and adoration to our Images, always questioning for [the] Blessed Mary, as men who have some knowledge or notice of this; and similar to our manner, they honor the Church, saying that between they and ourselves there is very little difference. These Bramenes [Brahmans] are naked from the waist upwards; from the waist downwards they cover themselves with some cotton cloths. They wear over the shoulder a thread of three *linhas*-strands which is the sign by which they are known as Bramenes. These are also men who do not eat anything which experiences death nor do they kill anything. They consider bathing a great ceremony, and they declare they are saved by this. These Bramenes, and thus the

112

Baneanes, marry after our manner, [i.e.] with only one wife, but one time, not more. In their wedding festivities they make great celebrations that last for many days, so that numerous people, very loudly celebrating the nuptials, come very well dressed and arrayed. For the greater part, they are married, thus men as women, [while] very young, and on the day which they must needs be received, the wedding couple are both seated on a dais, their persons very well arrayed in gold, precious stones and jewels. In front of them is a *mesquita* [lit. mosque but employed here in the sense of a temple] with an Idol covered with flowers [and] with many lamps of oil lit about it. In this place both [bride and groom] are obliged to be, with the eyes on that Idol, from morning until evening, without either one of them being allowed to eat, drink, or to speak. In the meantime they are well-feted by those people with plays of their instruments and with songs, firing many shots of the bombard, and likewise many rockets in making merry. And as they marry only once, if the husband dies, the wife (however youthful) does not marry again and vice versa. Their sons are their proper heirs, and in rank likewise, since Bramenes have to be sons of Bramenes. Among these [Gentiles] there are some of little worth who serve as messengers, and they proceed securely for all parts without molestation, even if a state of war exists, or if there are robbers. These people are called Pateles."

Livro de Duarte Barbosa

CHAPTER IX

DESCRIPTION OF THE CITY OF CAMBAY BY DUARTE BARBOSA

"Entering by Guandarim [Ghandhar], which is by the [Mahi] river inside [the Gulf of Cambay], there is a great and beautiful city that they call Cambay which is peopled by Moors and Gentiles. It has very good [and] very high houses, with windows, and they are covered by roofing tiles after our manner. The streets are very well layed out, with beautiful public squares, and noble buildings, all of stone and mortar. This city is situated in a gracious and rich land of provisions. The city possesses great merchants and great men of *fazendas*-revenues; thus Moors and Gentiles. It has many artisans of [the] mechanical offices, with subtle works of many fashions, thus as in Flanders, and all [are] very inexpensive. They manufacture many cloths of white cotton here, many being very thin and [others] thick, and others colored in proper form, and many cloths of silk, many inferior velvets of colors, many velvety satins, and taffetas, and many very large carpets.

"The natives of the land are nearly white, thus men as the women. Many foreigners live in the city and they are very white men. They are [a] very polished people and they are accustomed to many fine clothes, of [a] very luxuriant life, [one] given to many pleasures and sins. They eat very well. They are accustomed always to wash and anoint themselves with very sweet-smelling things. They always wear in their hair, thus men as women, flowers of jasmine and other grasses that the land possesses. They are great musicians of many manners of play and song. Carriages drawn by oxen proceed continually through the said city; and with horses which serve as portage for all kinds of things, and others with some very good *leitos*-bedsteads of wood, *sarados*-closed and covered in the manner of a chamber, carved with very beautiful *macenaria*-joinery and with windows armed and ornamented with many cloths of silk, and some with worked leather. In these are mattresses, bed covers, and very rich cushions of silk. Knowledgeable and trusted men drive [these carriages], whence they carry women to see games and amusements, or lady friends, without anyone being able to see or know who goes inside. Inside they proceed playing musical instruments and singing and doing all to their pleasure.

"The residents of this city have numerous meadowlands, gardens, and orchards, which serve as good places of relaxation, whence are nurtured many fruits, and garden greens, being [the] principal sustenance of those Gentiles who refuse to eat anything which has been killed.

"In this city a great sum of ivory is expended in works which are very subtly made and made with inlay, and other works of [the] lathe, such as bracelets, ends of daggers, and in *tresados*-broad swords, games *demxadres*-of chess, and tables, because in this place there are very skillful turners, who make all manner of things, and many *leitos*-bedsteads of ivory of [the] lathe, with many subtle designs, and beads of many manners, black, yellow, blue and red, and of many colors, which they carry from here for many parts; here there are great stone cutters and falsifiers of precious stones, and false pearls of many styles, which appear to be natural; it also has very excellent goldsmiths of very subtle works. Here they likewise make very beautiful bedspreads and canopies of beds, with very subtle workmanship and painting, and many quilted clothes for dress. It also has many Moorish lady *laurandeiras*-needlewomen, who make delicate and fancy needlework and subtle designs. Much coral is also cut here, and *alaquequas*-carnelians, and all kinds of other precious stones, in such a manner that this city has very prime artisans of all the crafts."

114

According to the time-worn view among scholars, Duarte Barbosa, the author of the book of the same name, was born in the city of Lisbon ca. 1480 and came to India in the squadron of Pedro Alvares Cabral in 1500, or possibly in the squadron of João da Nova in 1501, and lived in India until he returned to Portugal about the year 1518. In our time, however, Padre Schurhammer has denied that Duarte Barbosa, the author of the *Livro*, returned to Portugal in 1518, and indicates our author lived and died in India, and that the Duarte Barbosa who sailed with Magellan, and died with him in the Philippines in 1521, did not write the book which has been generally attributed to him, but that a second Duarte Barbosa wrote it.* Duarte Barbosa (whichever one) composed a work describing the peoples and lands of the Orient—from the East Coast of Africa to the Ryukyu Islands—which circulated in manuscript in India, and Gaspar Correa declares he saw it. Duarte Barbosa completed his book between the years 1516 and 1518. It was published posthumously, not in his native Portuguese, but in Italian, in the collection of voyages entitled *Delle Navigationi et Viaggi*, compiled by Giovanni Battista Ramusio, and published in Volume I of the said collection at Venice in 1550. A Portuguese manuscript was discovered at the beginning of the nineteenth century (not the original but a copy) and published under the title "Livro de Duarte Barbosa," *Collecção de Noticias para a Historia e Geografia das Nações Ultramarinas*, Tomo II Num. VII, Lisbon, 1813. The editors of the "Livro de Duarte Barbosa" have collated the Portuguese manuscript with the Italian version of Ramusio.

In the Preface to his work, published in the Italian version, Duarte Barbosa declares he sailed for many years of his youth over the seas of India (*nauigato gran parte della giouentu mia nella India*). We are not to doubt that he visited the Kingdom of Cambay during the period 1500-1518, and with the exception of Malabar, and possibly the Kingdom of Vijayanagar, Barbosa has described the Kingdom of Cambay in more detail, and with greater acumen, than any of the lands of Asia and Africa. From the vividness of his description of the city of Cambay, rendered above in full, we are justified in declaring Duarte Barbosa visited this city, although we are unable to support this averance with a positive statement from any source, or specify the particulars of his sojourn at Cambay, or assign a date to it.

CHAPTER X

DESCRIPTION OF THE CITY AND MOUNTAIN RANGE OF CHAMPANER BY JOAM DE BARROS

"This mountain range [of Champaner], by reason of a City situated at the foot of it, called Champanel [Champaner], has the same name. It is in the middle of some fields, and ascends to such a lofty altitude, that it appears to navigators from eighteen and twenty leagues at sea, being situated thirty leagues from the coast. The greater part of it is of such steepness, and with such jagged piles of great rocks,

---

* See Georg Schurhammer, "Doppelgänger in Portugiesisch-Asien," *Orientalia*, Rome and Lisbon, 1963.

that only by birds is it ascended. By another side, where
there are some ravines, it is enclosed by [a] wall, and close
by, a half a league away, is situated the City of Champanel
[Champaner] in a flat place, whose population is twenty
thousand inhabitants, with very noble buildings in which
there is a great traffic of merchants, and it is not enclosed
by walls. Close by this City runs a river that flows into the
Narbanda [Narmada] River, one of the greatest to enter the
Gulf of Cambay, and discharges its waters into the sea at the
City of Baroche [Broach].

"Departing Champanel [Champaner] to proceed to the
foot of the mountain range, that is to the place where one
ascends, there is a great and sumptuous temple that once
belonged to the Gentiles and now serves as a Mosque to the
Moors. From this temple a rampart departs from one side
and from the other, which serves as a road upon which to
proceed to the first enclosure that the mountain range has
near its foot. At the said place, on the part of the inside of
the first enclosure, there is a settlement as large as a substan-
tial Villa, containing two thousand Soldiers who guard that
entrance, and they keep watch by day and by night. And
close by the wall of the first enclosure, in suitable places,
are one hundred pieces of great artillery, and two hundred
artillerymen for the service of those pieces, the majority of
them [being] foreigners who have their wives and children
on the mountain range above, almost as hostages. Above this
enclosure, in a different part, there is another by [the] name
[of] Reguiguir, where there is settlement as great as the
Villa below, in which there are fifteen hundred Soldiers,
and fifty pieces of artillery, and twenty artillerymen, who likewise have wives and sons above. Its wall has three sentry
boxes and all in a mode of [an] excellent bulwark with its
artillery, and twelve catapults, and two *quartaos*, because the
site requires it. Proceeding up the mountain range, there is
another wall enclosed by a *cava*-trench cut from very rugged
rock, which in the winter [i.e. in the time of the Southwest
Monsoon, May to October] is filled with water, and over this
trench there is a drawbridge of wood, which they gather by
chains with capstans and retain in great hoops of brass which
are imbedded in the stones of the wall. The portal through
which they enter, and which serves this part, is so great,
that an elephant bearing his castle is able to pass through it.
It is lined with coverings of copper with great *laçarias*-
flourishes, inside and out, without the wood appearing to
which they are attached. On this wall are five great towers,
in each one of which are six pieces of artillery of the size of
our *esferas*, and along the wall are placed other small pieces
the size of our *falcões*, and four great *quartaos*, and eighteen

116

catapults. There are three thousand men in guard at this place, among which are counted five hundred musketeers and one hundred artillerymen who are all Rumes, *Mouros Garabijs* of this Africa, our neighbors, and Janizaries. These have their lodgings in some inferior houses along the wall.

"After the manner of these first three enclosures, there are three more, one above the other, so that on this mountain range there are altogether six whose upward slope is each time more defensible. Each one of these has trenches, bulwarks very well stored with artillery, artillerymen, and people ordered for its guard, and a settlement with great abundance of water, and all are provided with stores for more than three years; if any siege should endure as long. In the last of these six enclosures there is a great habitation, and to one side, the palaces of the Kings, which occupy a portion of ground, as great as that of a good-sized City, which are very richly wrought in ancient works of Mosaic, and relief, with great quantities of gold and silver, and [with] many houses ornamentally tiled in strange paintings and colors. In these palaces are many baths, and gardens, with all [the] diversity of trees, plants, fragrant herbs and flowers that the World possesses, and all manner of delights and pastimes. To one side are stables in which there are numerous horses for the King, and his people unsaddle them when they go there, with very rich saddles and harnesses. There the Kings have their wives, and their treasures, and the magazines for their arms and artillery, and the houses of manufacture for the latter, and provisions in great abundance. From these palaces of the King a secret passageway proceeds to the summit of the mountain range, upon whose pinnacle is another fortress provided with artillery in a grand manner with all the munitions and artifices of war necessary for its defense, and people of garrison, in which the Kings have yet other lodgings. Finally this is one of the strongest, most defensible and delightful locations in the World, thus by nature as by art, and [for the] riches which the Kings of Cambay have in it."

Da Asia, Decada IV Livro VI Capitulo IX

CHAPTER XI

DESCRIPTION OF THE CITY OF DIU BY DUARTE BARBOSA

The city of Diu is a great and opulent port situated upon a small island close by the *terra firma* of Cambay. To this port sail many *naos* from Malabar, Baticala (Bhatkal), Goa, Chaul, Dabhol and other ports. Likewise ships navigate from Diu for Ormuz, Aden, Mecca, Zeila, Berbera, Mogadishu, Brava, Melinde, Mombasa and other ports. The Malabares fetch coconuts, areca, pepper, ginger, cloves, mace, nutmeg, cinnamon, long pepper, sugar of Maticala (i.e. Baticala), *jagra* (sugar of palm-trees), emery, iron, wax, sandalwood and brazilwood to Diu, not to mention numerous silks and other commodities that come from Malacca and China. From Chaul and Dabhol come many *beirames*-calicos and *beatilhas*-fine muslins which are carried from Diu to Arabia and Persia. From Mecca and Aden copper, coral, quicksilver, cinnabar, lead, alum, gold, minted silver, *ruuia*-madder, saffron and rosewater come to Diu in great quantities.

The merchants who come to the port of Diu freight with many cloths of silk and cotton from the land; they load their ships with many horses, wheat, sesame, and sesame oil, opium from Aden, and opium from the Kingdom of Cambay; these merchants also carry many common camlets of silk, made in the Kingdom of Cambay, and which are very inexpensive, and from India many large carpets are brought to Diu, as well as noble taffetas, cloths of scarlet-in-grain (*panos de grãa*), other cloths in different colors, great quantities of spices and many other commodities, so that the port of Diu is now the chief emporium found in the parts of India, and possesses such a great store of money, that it is an astonishing thing—in the words of Duarte Barbosa—and this money has its source from the great quantities of merchandise that are loaded and unloaded at the port and city of Diu.

The king of Cambay has a governor of Diu called Malinquãs (Malik Aiyaz) who is an old man, yet a very good cavalier, and a industrious lord who conducts his affairs with great circumspection. Malinquãs (Malik Aiyaz) possesses very great artillery pieces to defend the port of Diu, and each day he manufactures new cannon. He likewise has many rowing vessels and an exceedingly strong bulwark lying across the entrance to his port, stored with very large artillery pieces and provided with many artillerymen for service of the cannon, who, with many men of arms, are continually on guard. They receive very good pay from the governor of Diu. The latter greatly fears the power of the king of Portugal. He makes great welcome to the Portuguese *navios* and people who proceed to the port of Diu. The people of the land are governed with justice.

Livro de Duarte Barbosa

CHAPTER XII

CAMBAY IN THE TIME OF THE EMPEROR AKBAR (1556-1605)
BY ABUL FAZL

The province (*subah*) of Gujarat (better known to us as Cambay) extends from Burhanpur to Jagat (Jakad) called Dwarka, a distance of three hundred and two kos,* and from Jalor in the north to Daman in the south, a distance of two hundred and sixty kos, and from Idar, likewise in the north, to Kambhayat (i.e. the city of Cambay), a distance of seventy kos. The land of Gujarat is watered by noble rivers: the Tapti, Narmada and the Sabarmati and others. The climate is temperate while the soil is sandy. The quality of the soil prevents the formation of mud during the rainy season. The principal nutriment of the people is *jowari* and *bajra*. The spring harvest is small. Wheat and certain food grains are imported from Malwa and Ajmer. Rice is imported from the Deccan. The prickly pear is planted in fields and gardens. The tree acts as a good fence. It is, however, a hindrance to travel across coun-

---

* A unit of Indian distance varying between one and three miles.

try. The land of Gujarat thus resembles a garden by reason of the numerous groves of mango and other trees. From Pattan (not to be confused with Pattan Somnath) to Baroda, a distance of one hundred kos, the land abounds with groves of succulent mango. Figs and muskmelon grow in Gujarat. Flowers and fruits are in great evidence. Grapes are found in moderation. The wilder regions of Gujarat are infested by the leopard.

There are innumerable artisans in Gujarat: painters, seal-engravers and other handicraftsmen. They inlay mother-of-pearl with great skill and make beautiful boxes and inkstands. Articles worked in gold thread are manufactured in these parts, and cloths of many varieties are skillfully manufactured. There are artisans who make excellent swords, daggers, and bows and arrows. The land conducts a lively trade in jewelry, and silver is imported from Turkey and Iraq. The houses of Gujarat are usually roofed with tiles and the walls are fashioned of burnt brick and lime. The vehicles of Gujarat are of two wheels drawn by two oxen. Pattan was once the capital of the province, and later Champaner and Ahmedabad.

Ahmedabad is a noble and prosperous city. It is virtually unrivalled for the salubrity of her climate and the excellence of her productions. The city possesses two forts and three hundred and sixty divisions denominated *pura* (a ward or city block). In the time of Abul Fazl, we are informed, eighty-four of these wards were in a flourishing state. There are one thousand stone mosques in the city of Ahmedabad, each with two minarets, and with rare inscriptions. Near Ahmedabad is the village of Sarkhech (Sarkhej) where Sultan Ahmed (1411-1442), who founded Ahmedabad, is buried. Indigo of good quality is grown near Ahmedabad and exported to Turkey and other countries.

> "Champaner is a finely situated fort on a crag of great height;
> the approach to it for two kos and a half is extremely difficult.
> Gates have been posted at intervals. At one place a cutting
> about 60 yards long has been made across which planks are
> laid which can be removed when necessity arises. Fine fruits
> abound."

Kambhayat (Cambay) is a large city. Merchants of many species live in this city. There are fine buildings and the city possesses a large commerce. At Pattan excellent cotton cloths are woven. They are carried to distant parts as gifts of value. Fine oxen are reared here and they are able to travel fifty kos in half a day. Pattan has two forts. Sorath (i.e. the peninsula of Kathiawar) is a land of grapes, melons, and numerous other fruits and flowers. Its climate is healthy. Excellent swords are made at Pattan Somnath.

"The Ain-i-Akbari," *Bibliotheca Indica*, Book III Ain 15.

CHAPTER XIII

DESCRIPTION OF THE KINGDOM OF MALWA, AND MORE PARTICULARLY, OF THE CITY OF MANDU, CAPITAL OF THE SAID KINGDOM, BY DIOGO DE MESQUITA

Diogo de Mesquita, the author of our description of the Kingdom of Malwa, was captured in a *batel* by a fleet of Diu in the year 1528, and from the port of Diu was carried prisoner to the king of Cambay (i.e. to Sultan Bahadur Shah, 1526-1537). Bahadur Shah demanded Diogo de Mesquita's conversion to the

Mohammedan religion, and when the latter refused to abjure his Christian faith, the sultan of Cambay threatened him with a cruel death. Diogo de Mesquita, however, endured all tortures of Bahadur Shah with constancy, being threatened, on one occasion, with being shot from a cannon, amongst lesser evils. Admiring his courage, the king of Cambay at last relented, and confined Diogo de Mesquita to a "sad" prison atop the mountain range of Champaner.

Diogo de Mesquita suffered imprisonment for many years, and we are informed by Gaspar Correa, that he learned to speak the Guzerate language at this time, and speaking with his guards, who allowed him great liberties, he diligenced for intelligence of Sultan Bahadur Shah and the exterior world, and occupied his leisure in writing a great *lenda* (i.e. a history, or account) of the affairs of Sultan Bahadur Shah and of Cambay, Malwa and the neighboring countries. The *lenda* of Diogo de Mesquita is no longer extant, but Gaspar Correa declares it circulated in India, and that he consulted it. With regard to Mandu, the capital of the ancient Kingdom of Malwa, Gaspar Correa extracted the following notice.

". . . in this Kingdom [of Malwa] there is a mountain called Mandou [Mandu], from which the Kingdom derived its name. The said mountain range was circular, of stout rock, denying combat save at the entrances that were narrow passageways cut in rock in flights of steps in regular advance, which one hundred men could defend against the entire world, and in altitude it would be two shots of [a] *falcão*. And neither by hunger or by thirst could it be taken, since the land on top was flat [and] verdant, fifteen leagues in breadth [alas 3 or 4 miles], with noble groves of trees and springs of water and game of many wild animals and birds. And it has fields for the sowing of rice and vegetables for [the] provision of ten thousand men, if so many were [needed] on the mountain range, and it has numerous settlements of people.

"Upon this range the King has his principal dwellings in many rich palaces where he has a reservoir of spring water, all carved in masonry with rich sculpture of white and black stones (in which there are many fish of all kinds), that was square, and was a quarter of a league [long] on each side; and close by this reservoir are the palaces, the best there are for the principal King of the world,[*] with noble buildings, sculptures and pictorial representations [for] all the houses and verandas, and inside splendid lodgings with rich chambers, with apartments for the King and his wives and sons, and surrounding the palaces [there are] lodgings for his captains and [the] officials of his house, for each one in great perfection, where the King was most of the time in luxury, where he possessed seven hundred women who shared

---

* The king of Malwa wanted a great deal of being the principal lord of Hindustan, let alone of the entire world.

120

his bed, all very beautiful [and] youthful women. Only one of these has the name of Queen, from whom are born the inheriting sons of the Kingdom, and the Queen is whosoever is first with child, being made *Rey*-king [alas Queen] by their custom. And the Queen is separated from the others, reigning and ruling as Queen, which is permitted to no other woman, who would be executed for this. The Queen is very powerful throughout the entire Kingdom. . . .

"And with the women of the mountain range the King has his pastimes of many songs, plays of instruments, and dances, and games, and above all with the mounted chase, to which the King proceeds in his litter, accompanied by these women dressed in riding apparel with Turkish bows, and arrows, and dogs. They are great *frecheiras*-lady archers, and beat the bush with dogs, and oblige the game to depart for the open country, where the King is with his huntresses placed in *paradas*-stations, who pierce and slay the game with arrows before the eyes of the King, who rewards whoever shoots the truest and who kills [the game] first."

Lendas da India, Tomo III Capitulo XLIII
Lenda de Nuno da Cunha

CHAPTER XIV

A NOTICE OF THE CITY OF CHITOR, OF THE ANCIENT RAJPUT KINGDOM OF THE SAME NAME, BY DIOGO DE COUTO

"This City of Chitor is in [a] latitude of nearly nineteen [alas 25] degrees of the North, according to the location that its natives give to it, and situated on top of a very high mountain range which nature has made so impregnable, that you can not climb it, save by one very steep way only, which is fortified by numerous and strong passes. The City is large, and enclosed by [a] beautiful wall, and with great and strong bulwarks, and so great by itself that it has benefit of sixty thousand persons, and the entire mountain range [is] so cool and pleasant that the natives gave it the name of Chitor, which some [Guzerates] say derives from a very beautiful *passaro*-bird found in that Kingdom, and of many colors, although other Guzerates declare that Chitor wishes to say *debuxo*-sketch."

Da Asia, Decada IV Livro IX Capitulo III

121

CHAPTER XV

AN ELEPHANT AND RHINOCEROS PITTED AGAINST EACH OTHER IN THE COURTYARD OF THE PAÇO DA RIBEIRA, LISBON—1515

"The Romans were accustomed to have condemned men fight one another in mortal combat, in places set aside for this, or with wild animals, or the same wild animals amongst themselves, for the greatness of the result. To these spectacles all who desired to see them came, and they were considered such mighty things that they relate them as things worthy of memory in their histories so that I would be deficient in this Chronicle if I neglected a kindred thing of the Romans, which the King Dom Manuel desired to effect in the city of Lisbon with an Elephant and a Rhinoceros. . . .

"Of these two wild animals the King Dom Manuel desired to see by trial the force and guile that each possessed in defending himself and attacking the other, for which in this year of fifteen hundred and seventeen, in the month of February,[*] he arranged to have them brought to a circuit, or [rather a] courtyard enclosed by high walls with battlements, being at that time in front of the house of contraction of India and Guinea, so that the Rhinoceros went first, which thus as it entered, they placed the animal behind some *pannos darmar*-hanging tapestries, hung upon a passageway leading from the room of the King to that of the Queen; and this so it would not see the Elephant enter from the door, and presently the Elephant entered; thereupon the men of the king's guard shut the doors of the courtyard.

---

* Damião de Goes has errored with respect to the date of this combat between the elephant and the rhinoceros, the same rhinoceros which King Muzaffar II, of Cambay, sent to King Manuel I, and which arrived at Lisbon on May 20th 1515 according to the testimony of an undated and unsigned letter (or rather an undated Italian copy; the original being lost) of Valentin Ferdinand (Valentim Fernandes) of Moravia to the merchants of Nuremberg (according to my guides). In this same letter Valentin Ferdinand of Moravia declares the elephant and rhinoceros were pitted against each other on the day of *Santa Trinita* (i.e. on June 3rd 1515) declaring he witnessed the spectacle. Vide also the "Alvará d'El-Rey D. Manoel em que manda a Ruy Leite entregar a João de Pina 2 barris, 2 picheis, 2 bacias de agua para as mãos, &." and the "Carta d'El Rey a D. Miguel da Silva," both published in the *Deambulações da Ganda de Modafar, Rei de Cambaia, de 1514 a 1516* by A. Fontoura da Costa. They are documentary engines without compeer, *a saber* that the fight between the elephant and the rhinoceros took place in 1515, and not 1517, and presumably on June 3rd as Valentin Ferdinand of Moravia indicates. The latter, we must note, has only consigned to record the particulars of the combat in precursory notice.

"These things concluded, the King ordered the hanging tapestries raised, where the Rhinoceros was hidden, which, although the creature was fettered (in which state it remained always), in seeing the Elephant, made a gesture towards the Indian who took care of it, and [who] conveyed it fastened by a long chain, as in [a] manner of asking to be allowed to proceed to where the enemy was; the Indian, because the beast now commenced to pull, extended the chain, nevertheless carrying the end in his hand, in such a manner, that with a very confident gait, it commenced to saunter for where the elephant was, the snout bent upon the ground, blowing through the nostrils with such force that it raised dust and straw from the ground as if there had been a gust of wind.

"The Elephant, when the Rhinoceros stepped forward, was back end to, but spying it, he turned around, bellowing trumpets, indicating with his trunk his desire to fight; however after the Rhinoceros approached close by, desiring now to attack his [the elephant's] belly, it appears for the little age that he had, he distrusted the efficacy of his tusks against such a mighty foe, for they were yet so little that they did not extend more than three spans beyond the mouth. He turned about, bolting straight for a grated window of iron that was close by the door of the courtyard, which *oulhaua*-faced the houses of the riverbank, upon which he placed the head with such force that he wrenched two *barões*-bars from the grating, that in thickness would be eight good inches in square, for between the said two bars he departed, leaving the Indian who governed him on the ground, who in this dilemma, threw himself from him, because if he had not done so he would have been crushed between the grating and the *lumear decíma*-upper sill of the window. This was one of the greatest displays of force that one could imagine.

"The Elephant having thus made his exit from the courtyard, bent his course for the [palace of] Estáos where he had his lodgings, not having regard for whatever he found in front, thus of men on foot, or of horses, so that he passed by everyone, making such a great tumult, that with the shouts of some to others, that they should be aware, it appeared that there had been a combat placed beyond its sphere, or [some] defeat by the enemy. It is worthy to note that the opening which the Elephant made between the two bars of iron, through which he passed, was so small that a man of common stature, dressed in [a] jerkin, with some difficulty would be able to pass through it. However the fear and industry of nature yielded the *getio*-motions which enabled him to wriggle through such a small place. The Rhinoceros remained very secure in the arena, almost as if to say to those who were near him, with the gestures and artful motions

123

which he made, that he had the victory for certain if the Elephant had cared to wait.

"The King Dom Manuel dispatched this same Rhinoceros, in the month of October of this year [1517 *] to Pope Leo X, and it embarked in a *nao* from Lisbon in which João de Pina, *cavalleiro* of his house, went for Captain, by whom also he sent to the Pope a very rich [set of] gilded silver tableware, cut in *bestiães*-animal work. The said *nao* went to Marseille [in January 1516 according to Antoine de Ruffi, Tome I Livre VII Chapitre V], where King François de Valois, the first king of France of that name, was at that time, [and] at whose entreaty João de Pina arranged to have the Rhinoceros placed on land so it might be seen, and he made service to him [to King François] by means of a very beautiful jennet, well *ageazado*-adorned, which the King accepted, and rewarded him with five thousand escudos of gold *do sol*. From Marseille he went to the coast of Genoa, where he was lost in a storm without anything being saved from the *nao*. The Rhinoceros came ashore dead where they flayed its hide, and it was carried to Rome and presented to the Pope stuffed with straw, which he saw and received with great surprise and sadness by reason of the loss of the people who went in the *nao* and [the] present that the King Dom Manuel dispatched to him."

---

* Again Damião de Goes has errored with respect to the date. From the "Alvará d'El-Rey D. Manoel em que manda a Ruy Leite entregar a João de Pina 2 barris, 2 picheis, 2 bacias de agua para as mãos, &." and the *Histoire de la Ville de Marseille* by Antoine de Ruffi, we apprehend João de Pina departed Lisbon en route to the Pope some time between October 1515 and January 1516, probably in November of 1515.

Crónica do Felicissimo Rei D. Manuel,
Parte IV Capitulo XVIII

BIBLIOGRAPHY

PRINTED SOURCES

1. Giovio, Paolo. *Dialogo Dell'Imprese Militari et Amorose*, Lyon, 1574.
2. Goes, Damião de. *Crónica do Felicissimo Rei D. Manuel*, Coimbra, Imprensa da Universidade, 1926.
3. Ruffi, Antoine de. *Histoire de la Ville de Marseille*, Marseille, 1696.

PUBLISHED DOCUMENTS

1. Costa, A. Fontoura da. *Deambulações da Ganda de Modafar, Rei de Cambaia, de 1514 a 1516*, Agência Geral das Colónias, Lisbon, 1937.
   a) Alvará d'El-Rey D. Manoel em que manda a Ruy Leite entregar a João de Pina 2 barris, 2 picheis, 2 bacias de agua para as mãos, &.— Lisbon, October 9, 1515: p. 38. Documento 3

b) Carta d'El Rey a D. Miguel da Silva—Lisbon, August 11, 1516: p. 41. Documento 6
2. Gubernatis, Angelo de. *Storia dei Viaggiatori Italiani nelle Indie Orientali*, Leghorn, 1875.
   a) Lettera scripta da Valentino Moravia germano a li mercatanti di Nurimberg, p. 389-392.

CHAPTER XVI

DESCRIPTION OF THE KINGDOM OF BENGAL BY JOAM DE BARROS

"The situation of the Kingdom of Bengal, of course, is in that part where the Ganges River discharges her waters by two principal arms into the Eastern Ocean, and moreover, where the land retreating from its waves, makes a great bay which the Geographers call *Gangetica*, and which we now call *Bengala*. At the mouths of the two arms of the Ganges, two notable rivers empty, one on the Eastern side, and the other on the Western, both being boundaries of this Kingdom; our people call one of these the [River of] Chatigam [Chittagong; i.e. the modern Karnafuli], as it enters the Eastern mouth of the Ganges at a City of this name, which is the richest and most celebrated [City] of that Kingdom, by reason of its port, at which the merchandise of all that Orient gathers. The other river enters the Western arm of the Ganges below another City called Satigam [Satgaon], likewise great and noble, but less frequented than Chatigam [Chittagong] since its port is less commodious for the entrance and departure of *naos*.

"The river of Chatigam [the Karnafuli] originates in the mountains of the Kingdom of Ava, and of Vagaru [apparently a lost kingdom of the Burmo-Indian border lands], and making its course from the Northeast for the Southwest, it divides the Kingdom of Bengal from the lands of Codovascan [Khuda Bakhsh Khan], and along the currents of this river lie the Kingdoms of Tipora [the ancient Kingdom of Tippera] and Brema Limma [unidentified, but east of Tipora according to the map of João Baptista Lavanha who edited Decada IV of João de Barros, after his death, and published his notes in 1615 (*editio princeps*) with a map of Bengal, among others]. They enclose Bengal from the side of the East.

"On the side of the North this Kingdom is encircled by some mountain ranges, which separate it from the Kingdom of Barcunda [the ephemeral Afghan Kingdom of Bihar *],

---

* Different accounts are offered by the Moslem historians of India as to the founding of the Afghan Kingdom of Bihar, among which the statements of the *Tarikh-i-Sher Shahi* of Abbas Khan are the most credible. He records one Bihar Khan assumed the kingship of Bihar with the title of Sultan Muhammad, following the defeat of Sultan Ibrahim, his master, by the Moguls in 1526 at the Battle of Panipat. The name "Bihar Khan" might appear to suggest the "Barcunda" of Barros, but the name he applies to the Afghan Kingdom of Bihar is traceable to the hill fortress of Bahrkunda (mentioned by Abbas Khan), to which Sher Khan, later Sher Shah, *de facto* ruler of Bihar in succession to Sultan Muhammad, retired—at times—during his wars with the

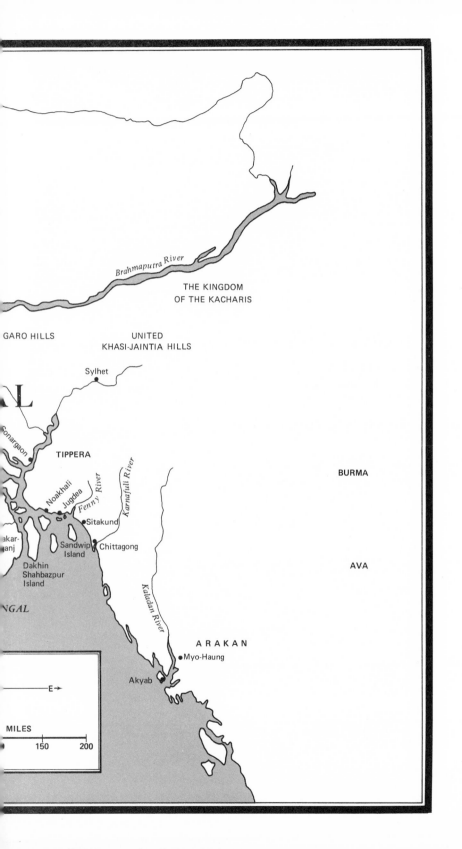

Brahmaputra *River*

THE KINGDOM
OF THE KACHARIS

GARO HILLS   UNITED
KHASI-JAINTIA HILLS

Sylhet

AL

Sonargaon

TIPPERA

BURMA

Noakhali
Jugdea   *Fenny River*   *Karnafuli River*

•Sitakund

akar-
anj

Sandwip   •Chittagong
Island

Dakhin
Shahbazpur
Island   AVA

NGAL   *Kaladan River*

ARAKAN
•Myo-Haung

E→

Akyab•

MILES

150   200

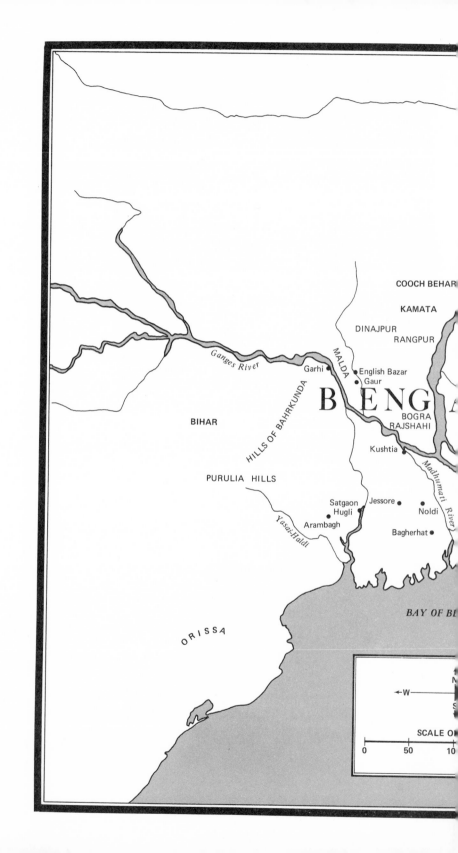

COOCH BEHAR

KAMATA

DINAJPUR
RANGPUR

Ganges River   Garhi •   MALDA
                                              • English Bazar
                                              • Gaur

BIHAR   BOGRA
                                              RAJSHAHI

HILLS OF BAHRKUNDA   Kushtia •   *Madhumati River*

PURULIA HILLS

                    Satgaon   Jessore •
                    Hugli   Noldi
Yasai-Haldi   Arambagh
                                  Bagherhat •

B ENG A

BAY OF BE

ORISSA

N
←W
S

SCALE O

0   50   10

among which nature has opened the way for that illustrious river Ganges to carry her waters to the sea. At this gap, which is at the extremity of this Kingdom, the King has a fortress called Gorij [Garhi] for [the] defense of the inhabitants of these mountains, and mountainous parts, through which the Ganges River debouches, so that [no enemy] will be able to enter by land or by water. These same mountain ranges, proceeding Westwards, divide the people of Bengal from the Patane people [i.e. the Pathans or Afghans of the Kingdom of Bihar], and beyond, [they proceed] towards the south of the Kingdom of Orixa [Orissa], remaining the plains of Bengal between these mountain ranges and the current of the Ganges River. Another river, which enters the Ganges below Satigam [Satgaon], runs through the Kingdom of Orixa, and has its sources behind the mountain range which the Indians call Gate [i.e. the Ghats], in that part where it borders with Chaul; and as this river is great, and runs through many lands, the natives in imitation of the *Ganges*, in which it discharges, also call it *Ganga*, and consider its waters sacred, as those of the Ganges. [*] In this manner the Kingdom of Bengal lies in its maritime parts, that is, to the south between the two rivers, this of Satigam to the West, and that of Chatigam to the East, and the two arms of the Ganges, in which they flow, forming the figure of the Greek letter Delta, as do all the great rivers which enter the sea in mouths.

"The entire land between one arm, and the other, is divided into Islands, or Fluvial Meadowlands, which have been cut by the waters of the same Ganges, and of the other great rivers that enter it; so that commencing from the Eastern mouth, these are the names which have come to our notice: Tranquetea, Sundiva [Sandwip], Ingudia, Merculij, Guacalan, Tipuria, Bulnei, Sornagam, Angara, Mularangue, Noldij,

---

Mogul Emperor Humayun. Why Barros chose to denominate the Kingdom by the name of this obscure fortress I do not, since I can not offer explanation. Sher Khan conquered the independent Kingdom of Bengal in 1538, and at his death in 1545, he ruled nearly all of northern India with the exception of the Kingdom of Cambay. He was the last resolute Afghan Emperor of India, and after his death and that of his son, Islam Shah (1545-1553), the Moguls erected their dominion in India upon a secure foundation and ruled India until the dissolution of their empire in the 18th century.

---

* It appears from the map of João Baptista Lavanha, that Barros is referring to the Haldi River, amongst others, but his geographical notices are faulty, since the sources of the Haldi River are discovered amongst the Purulia hills, and not in the mountains behind Chaul.

Cupitavaz, Pacuculij, Agrapara and many others.[*] Within the limits that we conceive as the boundaries of the Kingdom of Bengal, these Kingdoms are subject to it: Caor [situated by João Baptista Lavanha astride the river Caor (i.e. the Brahmaputra) behind a chain of mountains, corresponding to the modern Garo and United Khasi-Jaintia Hills in Assam, and which I believe is the ancient kingdom of the Kacharis], which marches with the Kingdom [of] Cou [Cooch Behar], and at another time was part of it, and the Bengalis usurped it, and below it in the direction of the sea, the Kingdom of Comotaij [Kamata], and another called Cirote [Sylhet] where they make all the eunuchs that come to Bengal, and go to divers parts, of which it has [a] great number. The state of Codavascam [Khuda Bakhsh Khan], who is a Moorish Prince, [a] great lord, with his abode between Bengal and the Kingdom of Arracam [Arakan], the Bengalis reckon within the bounds of their Kingdom, and thus that of Tipora [Tippera]; but as these are mountainous, the Bengalis declare that certain powerful lords revolted with these lands against the King of Bengal, and since between the *Tiporitas* and the *Bengalas* there has always been rancor, and emulation, as is usually the case between neighboring Kingdoms when some pretend to be greater than the other, or superior, the *Tiporitas* formed a league with those of the Kingdom of Cou, likewise enemies of [the] Bengalis, so that they revolted against them, and since this Kingdom of Cou is great, and has more horsemen than any of its neighbors, and is rugged by reason of the many mountain ranges which it possesses, by itself it would be able to conquer Bengal, and so more readily with the help of the *Tiporitas*, who are [a] very bellicose people. But as these two allied and confederated Kingdoms are Gentile, without allowing Moors amongst them, who with artillery, and [the] artifices of war which they employ, have made the Kingdom of Bengal powerful, these two allied Kingdoms have nearly come to be lost, as they lack the military discipline of the Moors, who dominate them, although they tower above them in spirit, prowess and valor.

"On the other side of the West, against the Kingdom of Orixa [Orissa], the Bengalis possess the Kingdom of Cospetir

---

* The delta of the Ganges has undergone so many changes within the past four hundred years, that to attempt to identify these islands is attended by every element of presumption, and conversely, wanting in every element of exact science, that I forbear rendering aids to the reader in this direction, save in the instance of Sundiva. Vide, however, H. Blochmann, "Contributions to the Geography and History of Bengal (Muhammadan Period)," *Journal of the Asiatic Society of Bengal*, Calcutta, 1873, where the attempt is made.

[Gajpati], whose plains are covered by the Ganges in the time of the floods almost in the manner of the Nile; and since Bengal the greater part of the time contends with two neighboring Kingdoms, with that of Orixa, which is Gentile, and with the Patanes [Pathans], of whom the greater part are Moors, that Kingdom [of] Cospetir is trampled upon when they enter, until those Patanes totally dominated it as the lords of the land. . . .

"Of this Kingdom of Bengal, and of four others, her neighbors, the Gentiles and Moors of those parts, say that God gave to each one its particular gift; to Bengal people on foot without number; to the Kingdom of Orixa [Orissa] elephants; to that of Bisnaga [Vijayanagar] many dexterous people with the sword and shield; to the Kingdom of Delhi many Cities and villages; and to it of Cou great numbers of horse. To those thus named in this order, they give other names: Espatij, Gaspatij, Noropatij, Buapatij and Coapatij.

"The land of Bengal, as it lies between twenty-two and twenty-seven degrees of the part of the North, and the greater part consists of fields washed by four notable rivers, and is cut into meadowlands (as we said), all is very fecund, not only with rice, which is their general sustenance, but with many vegetables, greens and fruits, like those of our Hispania, and others which we do not have in these parts, that are native to those regions of the Orient. Throughout this entire Kingdom they make great quantities of good *assucar*-sugar, that they carry in bundles for other parts. A good deal of long pepper is found there, and it is bountiful with all kinds of great and small livestock, and wild animals, and birds of the river bank of all kinds. It nurtures many horses of the size of *facas*-hackney horses of England, and they pick so much cotton, and the land has so many Artisans, that they weave very fine cloths, so that they might dress the whole of Europe with them, because not only from Malacca, and beyond, in which there are an infinite number of Islands in that Archipelago, but yet throughout all of India, upon whose coast, in all the places, they make an infinite number of cotton cloths, since the common run of people do not dress with another thing, whoever wishes to dress with fine cloths, is obliged to have those of Bengal; and in the things of workmanship of [the] needle, and differences of patterns, among all those people, the Bengalis carry the advantage, as one may observe in the fancy needlework of the very rich bed spreads, and of other things which come from that place.

"For the most part, the native people of the land are Gentiles, weak for war, but the most malicious and treacherous [people] in the entire Orient, so that to slander a man in whatever part, it suffices to say that he is a Bengali. But

129

these people have one blessing, that as they are [a] people who do not have more of theirs than what they gather to eat that day, in this poverty they are more secure in life than the grandees, because these, as they are weighed with the goods of the world, presently they are found at fault, so that they are seized for the King, and often they lose their lives with their possessions; and when they die a natural death, the King is heir, thus of the rich, as of the indigent. The King employs another tyranny, that as his Officers of the justice, and of the revenues, have occupied their offices for a time, and if it appears to him that amongst them one is already great in wealth, for whatever defect, he calls him, and by the agency of lashes, he takes from him what he can, and then they dress him [in] a *cabaia*-Turkish tunic, which the King bestows, with which he departs more honored than abused by those lashes, for it is a sign that he is now reconciled with the King, and with that honor of the *cabaia*-Turkish tunic he dispatches him to serve in his office; so that once again he robs him, since he [the office holder] knows he deserves yet other lashes."

Da Asia, Decada IV Livro IX Capitulo I

CHAPTER XVII

NOTICES OF THE CITY OF GAUR FROM DUARTE BARBOSA

"The Moors [of the Kingdom of Bengal] live by the ports of the sea, for which there is [a] great trade in many varieties of merchandise and they sail *naos* and *navios* for many parts, since this sea is a bay which enters between two lands; and proceeding a good distance upon it, this [sea] has [towards] the north a very great city peopled by Moors which they call Bengala [i.e. Gaur; today in ruins]; a very good port of [the] sea [in communication with the Bay of Bengal by means of the river Ganges]. It has [a] Moorish King standing by himself. The residents are white men, [and] well-formed. From many parts numerous foreigners have also come to live there, to wit, Arabians, Persians, Abyssinians and Indians; and these since the land is very great, rich, healthy and temperate.

"All are very great merchants, and they have great *naos* of the fashion of Mecca, [and] others of China which they call junks, that are very noble and load very great cargos, with which they navigate for Coromandel, Malacca, Sumatra, Pegu, Cambay and Ceylon. They trade with many varieties of merchandise for these and many other parts. In this city there are many cottons, great *canaueaes*-cane fields of very good sugar, ginger and long pepper. Many kinds of extremely fine and colored cloths for dress are fashioned here, and moreover white cloths for merchandise, which they carry to many parts. They possess great value, and some, which they call *estrauantes*, which is a type of thin cloth, are greatly esteemed by us for *touquados de donas*-lady's headpieces, and by the Moors, Arabians and Persians for *touquas*-turbans. Of these they manufacture such a quantity that they freight many *naos* with them for trade abroad. Besides these they manufacture others which they call *mamonas*, others [called] *duguazas, chautares* [and] *sinabafas*, which are the best, and moreover the Moors esteem them for shirts [i.e. for jibbas]. All these varieties of cloths are in pieces, each one being twenty-three [and] twenty-four Portuguese *varas* [one *vara* equals 43.31 inches] in length. They are very inexpensive. They are spun on wheels by men, and woven by them. In this city they also manufacture much and good white sugar from canes, but they do not know how to join it and make loaves of bread; and thus as powder they bundle it in some very well fastened sacks of rawhide. A great sum of these [sacks] are freighted, which they carry for sale to many parts, because it is [a] very great merchandise. When these merchants are accustomed to come freely, and without fear to Malabar and Cambay with their *naos*, a quintal of sugar in Malabar is worth one thousand and three hundred reis, and a very good *chautar* six hundred reis, and a *sinabafa* two cruzados and a piece of very good *beatilha*-fine muslin three hundred reis, which things they bring, and selling them, they gain a good deal. In this city they also manufacture conserves of ginger, oranges, lemons and other fruits which originate in this land. Here are found many horses, cows, sheep, and many other kinds of livestock in abundance, and many chickens.

"The Moorish merchants of this city often depart for the interior to buy Gentile lads from their fathers and mothers, and they steal others, and they are castrated, and they remain entirely shorn; many die from that; those who escape are educated very well, and they sell them. They are greatly esteemed as guards for their women and *fazendas*-estates, and for other vile things, for which these eunuchs are respected, since they are men of great dispatch, and come to be factors of their lords, and governors and captains of the Moorish Kings, in such a manner that they become very rich men with great *fazendas*-revenues.

"The respected Moors of this city are dressed with some white shirts [jibbas] of very fine cloth of cotton, falling to the ankle, and beneath, some cloth wrapped around the body, and above some *maxilares*-bands of silk, their daggers at the waist, garnished in silver and gold, in accordance with the rank of the man who bears it. [They wear] numerous rings upon the fingers with very precious stones, [and] their *fotas*-turbans of cotton upon the head. They are very luxuriant, who eat very well, and spend without fear, and in addition to these things, they have many other vices. They bathe themselves very often in great tanks which they have inside their houses. Each one possesses three or four wives, or as many as they can support, which they keep well secluded. And they treat them very well, with great quantities of gold, and silver, and rich cloths of silk. They do not leave [their compounds] except at night to visit, some amongst others, whence they make many fetes and wedding feasts, with [a] superfluous diversity of wines, of which they manufacture in this land many kinds, principally of sugar from palm trees, of which their wives are greatly addicted. The women are great musicians of many modes of play with instruments. The rabble of this city dress in some little white shirts, ex-tending to mid-thigh, and on their heads [they wear] some very little turbans with three or four turns. In their foot-wear they have good cordovan leather, for their shoes; others [wear] sandals well worked and covered. The King is [a] very great and rich lord of [a] noble and well populated land. The Gentiles turn Moors in these parts every day so as to be favored by their governors."

Livro de Duarte Barbosa

CHAPTER XVIII

NOTICES OF THE CITY OF GAUR FROM JOAM DE BARROS

"The principal City of this Kingdom [of Bengal] is called Gouro [Gaur], situated on the banks of the Ganges; and they say it is three Portuguese leagues in length, and [that it has] two hundred thousand inhabitants. It has the river as [its] enclosure on one side, and on the landward side, a very high wall of stone and mortar, and at the part away from the river, a *cava*-trench full of water, upon which great *bateis* are able to float. The roads are wide and straight, and the principal streets have trees arranged in order along the *paredes*-walls[?] so as to provide shade to those who pass that way; and as the people are numerous, the roads are so crowded with the traffic and service of people, principally those which proceed for the palaces of the King, that some are unable to pass, for which those who fall amongst the people on horseback, or upon elephants, on which the Lords and noblemen ride, are very often crushed and killed beneath the feet of these animals. [A] great part of the houses of this City are noble, and well wrought; and the riches and extent of the trade of this City, and of all the Kingdom of Bengal was so great, before the Patanes [Pathans] captured it . . . that Sultan Badur [Bahadur, 1526-1537], being himself one of the richest Kings in that Orient, and very arrogant, used to say that he was one, and the King of Narsinga [Vijayanagar] two and the King of Bengal was three, meaning to say that the King of Bengal had alone, as much as he, and the King of Bisnaga [Vijayanagar] had together."

Da Asia, Decada IV Livro IX Capitulo I

CHAPTER XIX

NOTICES OF THE CITY OF GAUR FROM FERNAM LOPES DE CASTANHEDA

"There are many and very beautiful cities situated along the Ganges from one part to another, principally one that is called Gouro [Gaur], which is one hundred leagues up river from the sea. It is well made; four leagues in length; and the width is little. Although [the land] is flat it [Gaur] is very strong since the Ganges encloses it in front, and behind [there is] a great and deep *alagoa*-lagoon, in which *naos* of four hundred tons float. And back of this *alagoa* there are jungles that nurture many elephants, tigers, *onças*-leopards and other wild animals. Because these jungles fortify the city, the kings of Bengal do not wish them cut, and for this reason they are very thick. In them there are many and noble buildings, such as mosques and houses of [the] lords that attend the court of the king of Bengal, who has his residence in sumptuous palaces that are of the dimensions of the city of Evora;[*] these buildings are low lying wrought with gold and with bluish tiles (*azul*), and they have numerous courtyards and gardens, and a good store of provisions. It is peopled by Moors and Gentiles, and many foreigners live

---

* A twenty minute walk suffices to carry one through the main gate of Evora, coming from the railroad station, to a gate on the other side of the city, by a small park. Evora is a pleasant mediaeval city, built on a small hill, and surrounded by a mediaeval wall. I noticed very little expansion of the city beyond the ancient limits when I visited Evora on February 5th 1968.

there, including Persians, as well as Khurasanis, Rumes and Abyssinians, who, coming with their merchandise, decided to remain there seeing the greatness of the land."

História do Descobrimento & Conquista da India pelos Portugueses, Livro IV Capitolo XXXVII

". . . the houses of the king, which are of the dimensions of Evora, [are] a sumptuous and noble construction; all the houses are worked with embellishments of gold, and the floors and the walls covered with ornamental tiles; and in the middle of these palaces is a courtyard which occupies as much space as the *resio*-Rossio[*] of Lisbon, which is entered by twelve gates, and all in turns, and at each one four door men are stationed, and at the end of this courtyard is a veranda—which they call Baileu—where the King of Bengal hears ambassadors, at which time the courtyard is full of people of arms. These palaces also have many gardens and *casas de prazer*-pleasure houses, which besides being sumptuous are very delightful."

História do Descobrimento & Conquista da India pelos Portugueses, Livro VIII Capitolo LXVII

CHAPTER XX

NOTICES OF THE CITY OF GAUR FROM AN ANONYMOUS MANUSCRIPT PRESERVED IN THE TORRE DO TOMBO, LISBON, IN THE COLLECTION ENTITLED *SAM VICENTE*

"In these days that we were thus at leisure [i.e. after Gonçalo Tavares had rendered his embassy and before the dispatch of the Portuguese from Gaur; See Chapter II Section 6], I departed some times for this city to know what [kind of] land it was and its customs. The city is large. Along the river it extends for four leagues and towards the interior they say it is so great that the populated area extends for more than six leagues. However I did not see the interior, nor do I know how far it extends. I saw only that the land is very fruitful and has many groves of trees and great fields of sugar. It has great numbers of *rabaos*-plants of rape and cabbage, and many other fruits of the land, and [the] location of the city is upon a very great flat plain because all the land is such. All the cross roads are paved with bricks as the new road in Lisbon, and along all these roads and byways are great crowds of people, at which all things are sold in abundance, thus of provisions, as of all [other]

---

* With the Praça do Comércio, the Rossio is the great square of Lisbon. It occupies as much space as a good football field, sidelines included.

things, and all very inexpensively, and the number of people is so great, that you are unable to go by road or byway because of them, in such a manner that the great lords, as they come or go from the palace, are wont to carry men with canes in front of them, and with blows, they force the people aside, and if they did not do it, they would not be able to pass, although they kill many people beneath the feet of the horses and elephants, of which the land has many.

"The majority of [the] people of which I speak are so poor that they lack sufficient food and dress, and the chief part of them wear *lyteyros*-sack cloth and others *esteyras*-coarse cloth. Thus when the winter commences, so many of these people die, that the roads are full of them in the morning, because the land is so cold from the first of November until the beginning of March, that they are not able to maintain themselves save those that have the wherewithal to buy firewood and to make great fires as we make here in Portugal . . . [here follows a description of how the Moors seized the Kingdom of Bengal from the Gentiles—falsely based on hearsay. Our author declares he was told these things by certain Arabian and Persian merchants] . . .

"Order of the city: the roads are all *arruadas*-straight and in good order, and there are certain roads where all manner of arms are sold, thus of swords and lances, as skirts of mail, and buff-coats with their steel laminae, and thus plated helmets, and thus there are saddle shops where they sell saddles and sundry accoutrements for horses and here there is [a] road for merchants where they sell all the cloths of silk and of other colors.

"Order of the King: the King has five hundred *fidalgos* and sons of dukes and great lords for his guard. These guard the inside of the palaces and also [they keep guard] when he departs to go outside, and he has, moreover, two thousand and five hundred men of guard who are always with the great flag of which I have already spoken [See Chapter II Section 6], because the *lasquarys*, about whom I have written above, are vassals of the *allferez*-ensign who brings the flag.

"I went inside their stables. In the said stables I counted four thousand and five hundred horses, *a saber*, one thousand and five hundred for his own person, and for which he makes rewards to the great lords, and the [remaining] three thousand are for the men of his guard and for his valets and pages of which the majority are eunuchs.

"I went in the elephant stable where I counted nine hundred and fourteen, all of war, who are trained to fight with swords tied to their tusks and with their trunks they throw assagais so that they kill and injure many people, and among these elephants of which I speak, there are three of the

135

King's own person, and amongst these three there is one that has the right shoulder with the fore-foot free and the left shoulder with the leg entirely red, like blood, and the trunk stained with these same colors, and the tusks are so thick as a man around the waist, and this elephant when he comes to a *quadea*-chain which is in front of the palaces, that is as great as I have related above, if it is not presently lowered for him, he raises his trunk and breaks it in pieces, and when the King has occasion to ride upon him, he places himself on the ground and extends his trunk, upon which the King places his foot, and with it, he puts him [the king] upon himself.

"The King has two thousand and five hundred women. These are the daughters of the principal men of the land, and they are [lodged] in some compartments inside these same palaces. They are guarded by eunuchs who have charge to give them all necessary things, each one as she needs it, and he has, moreover, three thousand wives that remain from his father, who he sends to give all things necessary.

"Each one of the great lords has fifteen and twenty wives, each one of which he maintains in his house, and there they are provided with everything necessary, since in this place it is not customary to legitimate sons, because as one proves to be his son, he inherits presently his share of the property, which property by the death of the fathers, the King will inherit half and the wives and sons the other half.

"One day I found myself at the door of a mosque that is on a great plain, as I was hunting with a *besta*-crossbow, and I saw [a] very great number of people come and I asked who those people were, and knew that the King came to give alms for the soul of his father, and so as to know what he gave, I desired to spend that day there, and moreover of the alms given, I knew from the rolls of forty scriveners, who wrote he had given three *laiques* of *tangas* of the land and two *laiques* in clothes making in sum five thousand cruzados.

"And presently at another day (*a outro dya*) they told me that the King would give things to eat for the soul of his mother, and I went to see it, or how he would do it, and I saw in that same field one hundred and fifty cars loaded with cooked rice, and many loaves of bread, and *rabaos*-turnips and onions and figs and many other fruits of the land, and another fifty carts loaded with cooked and roasted beef and mutton, and thus great supplies of fish, also cooked, all to give to the poor.

"All this food that he distributed cost in sum as money. These things having been concluded, he gave six hundred thousand [of] our *tangas*, each *tanga* being three *vintens*, for which I remained very surprised, and I should not have believed it, if I had not seen it, and this money that he gave was thrown from atop a scaffold above all the people, who numbered four or five thousand."

Lembrança dalgumas coussas que se passaram quando Amtonio de Bryto e Dyogo Pereyra foram a Bemgalla asy em Bengala como em Tanaçaiym e em Pegu onde tambem fomos, São Vicente, Vol. 11—Folhas 61r.-65r.

CHAPTER XXI

BENGAL IN THE TIME OF THE EMPEROR AKBAR (1556-1605) BY ABUL FAZL

The province (*subah*) of Bengal extends from Chittagong to Garhi, a distance of four hundred kos, and from the mountains of the north to the district (*sarkar*) of Mandaran (near modern Arambagh), a distance of two hundred kos. The countries of Arakan, Tippera and Cooch Behar (*Kuch*) march with Bengal on the one side, and Bihar and Orissa upon the other.

The heats of summer are moderate. The cold season is of short duration. The rains commence in May, and endure for more than six months. During the rainy season the plains are flooded; specially constructed ridges rise above the waters.

The rivers of Bengal are innumerable. Foremost is the river Ganges. Its source is not known. Rising in the mountains of the north, it flows through the province of Delhi, thence Agra, Allahabad, Bihar, into the province of Bengal, whence it divides in the district (*sarkar*) of Barbakabad (comprising the modern districts of Rajshahi, Southwest Bogra and Southeast Malda). One arm, flowing eastwards, falls into the sea near Chittagong. The other arm spreads into many channels and flows southwards. From its source, as far as the sea, the Ganges is considered to be sacred by the Hindus. Its waters are carried to distant places. The Hindus consider the worship of the Ganges to be an act of adoration of the supreme being. "Its sweetness, lightness and wholesomeness attest its essential virtues." The Brahmaputra flows from China (*Khata*) through the Kingdom of Cooch Behar (*Kuch*). Its waters fertilize the land of Bengal. The Brahmaputra also falls into the sea.

The principal crop of Bengal is rice of which there are numerous varieties. Rice is sown and reaped three times a year on the same piece of ground. The crop is little injured by it. The harvests are abundant and revenue demands are determined by the estimate of the crop. The common food is rice and fish. Considering wheat and barley unwholesome, the Bengalis do not esteem these crops. The people are submissive and pay their rents.

As a rule the people, thus men as well as women, wear only a loincloth. Their houses are constructed of bamboo. Travel is by boat, especially during the rainy season. The Bengalis have different varieties of craft as the occasion offers. Thus they have boats for war, transport and for swift-sailing. On land they employ a *sukhasan* or a crescent-shaped litter covered with camlet or scarlet cloth, and the like. The *sukhasan* is constructed for either sitting, lying or sleeping. A cover is provided for protection against the sun and rains. It is remov-

137

able at will. Some of the natives ride elephants. Few, however, ride horses. Salt is in great demand and is carried to Bengal from afar. Diamonds, emeralds, pearls, carnelians and agates are also imported. There are numerous fruits and flowers in the land. Cloths of different varieties are produced.

"Jannatabad is an ancient city. For a time it was the capital of Bengal and was widely known as Lakhnauti and for a while as Gaur. His Majesty the late Emperor Humayun distinguished it by this title of Jannatabad. It has a fine fort and to the eastward there is a lake called Chhatiapatia containing many islands. Were the dam that confines it to break, the city would be under water. About a kos to the north of the fort, is a large building and a reservoir, monuments of great antiquity. From time immemorial, its water has been considered to be of a poisonous character. The place was called Piyasbari, and criminals condemned to death, were confined there, who, in a short time, perished from the effects of this brackish water. At present in the blessed reign of His Majesty [the Emperor Akbar], this practice has been discontinued."

In the *sarkar* of Ghoraghat (comprising the modern districts of South Rangpur, Southeast Dinajpur and North Bogra) silk and a type of sackcloth are produced, and eunuchs and hill ponies are procurable. The *sarkar* of Sylhet furnishes many eunuchs. Aloeswood is found abundantly in the mountains of Arakan. It is situated by the sea, being an excellent port, and is surrounded by woods. It is the resort of Christians (i.e. the Portuguese) and other merchants. In the *sarkar* of Satgaon two ports are situated half a kos from each other: Satgaon and Hugli, of which the latter is the chief port. Both are in the possession of the Europeans (i.e. of the Portuguese). Fine pomegranates are grown here.

"The Ain-i-Akbari," *Bibliotheca Indica*, Book III Ain 15.

CHAPTER XXII

DESCRIPTION OF THE KINGDOM OF DELHI BY DUARTE BARBOSA

The Kingdom of Delhi is a great kingdom in the interior of India, marching with Tartary on the side of the north, with many lands of great and rich cities. It is peopled by both Moors and Gentiles. The king of Delhi is a Moor by religion and a very great lord of numerous warlike people. Formerly the Kingdoms of Cambay and Deccan belonged to the king of Delhi, but they revolted when he dispatched some captains to complete the conquest of those kingdoms. In ancient times the Kingdom of Delhi belonged to the Gentiles of India, and there are many Gentiles who live very wretchedly in this land of Delhi. Many are noble and honorable men, who, to avoid the subjugation of the Moors, take *abitos proues*-poor habits, and proceed on long peregrinations until they die.

The Moors and Gentiles of the Kingdom of Delhi are good warriors and fine cavaliers. They are equipped with many kinds of weapons. They are sturdy men and excellent archers. They have very good lances, swords, tiny hatchets and maces of steel with which they engage in combat. They are always wont to wear some disks of steel, which they call *Chaçaram*, two fingers in width, as sharp as razors on the outside, and blunt on the inward side. These disks are as large as a small *pratel*-plate and they are bored. Each warrior carries up to ten of these upon his left arm, and when at war they take one of these disks and placing it on the fingers of the right hand, and bringing the arm back to gather force, they throw these disks at the enemy with great force, and if it strikes a man's arm, or leg, or lodges in the neck, they cause grave injuries, and thus these disks do great damage to an enemy force. In the Kingdom of Delhi there are men very skillful with these disks.

In the Kingdom of Delhi there are some trees whose root they call *Braechagua*, and this root is so venomous that who or whatever eats it, dies from its poison. However the fruit of this same plant, which they call *Miralexy*, possesses the virtue of killing the poison of the root, and other poisons besides, and gives life to a man who has eaten this root. Those Gentiles who wander in peregrinations carry the root and the fruit and some of these Gentiles give these things to the kings of India.

Livro de Duarte Barbosa

APPENDIX I

THE VOYAGE OF GIOVANNI DA EMPOLI, AND RAFAELLO GALLI, CITIZENS OF THE REPUBLIC OF FLORENCE IN SERVICE OF THE KING OF PORTUGAL, TO DIU—1515-1516

EXTRACT OF THE LETTER OF RAFAELLO GALLI TO HIS UNCLE, GIOVANNI DA POPPI, SECRETARY OF THE MAGNIFICENT LORENZO DE'MEDICI IN THE CITY OF FLORENCE

Dated Pacem, 10th-20th September 1516

"We departed on the 16th of November [of 1515] for Cambay [with] Messer Giovanni [da Empoli as] captain of a *nave* called *Belem*, [a] *nave* of 600 tons, and factor of it and of two other *nave* and all at his command, and thus we departed for those ports well favored; and our sojourn was at Diu, [a] land of very great trade and rich merchandise. The lord of the said land is called Melegias [Malik Aiyaz], [a] great lord and [a] Moor. The said was always [a] great friend of Messer Giovanni and made great favor to him and every day he was pleased to speak with him and give dispatch to his merchandise in the three *nave*; thus he sold one hundred and twenty thousand ducats worth of goods. He amazed the people with the great quantity of merchandise that he carried; and all passed very well and he richly loaded the said *nave*, and principally his [ship], with all the rich merchandise that they could hold. And with many rich presents, he departed the second day of *Pasqua di Resurressa* for India so as to pass this year upon our voyage to the island of *Zamatera*-Sumatra, which would be in good hour. We arrived at *Chocim*-Cochin at so many days of April and Messer Giovanni was very well noticed by the Governor of India [Lopo Soares de Albergaria] and well favored by him and by the other captains, and he was given the said *nave* *Belem* in order to proceed upon our voyage."

"Lettere di Giovanni da Empoli e di Raffaello Galli," *Archivio Storico Italiano*, Florence, 1880. Documento Numero IV.

APPENDIX II

LETTER OF THE KING OF BENGAL TO THE KING OF PORTUGAL

From the City of Bengal (i.e. Gaur),
Without date

"All my love and my blessing and good will. Powerful King of Portugal, just lord of the land and of the sea. Designated King for all parts of the world, in Christendom, in Persia, in Arabia, well-known and had for lord of great power with the aid of God, and lord of great wisdom, with great fame, and beloved by all for your works.

"Your Highness will know, very powerful lord, that one your captain, Dom João, came to a port which is near this city of Bengal, called Aque Cama [unidentified], with four *naos* and he sent a *batel* to this city where I am now, with great friendship, which I have desired for a long time, and I was greatly pleased with him [with his messenger?] for the news [he brought], because I have hoped for so much. Presently I offered to him all my power, and the city, and generally what would be suitable to the service of Your Highness, for which we remain very good friends with great [good] will; nevertheless I remain somewhat fearful until I see the will of Your Highness.

"Your Highness will know that Joanes, factor, came to a port near this city of Bengal, called Quylaa, who came in a *nao* of the land with a merchant of it, and one Fernando, and they gave me a *carta de segurança*-letter of safe-conduct, and he did not desire to trust me, and I desired to send it to Dom João, because I am distrustful until I see the will of Your Highness.

"Your Highness will know that I do not wish more of him than for Your Highness to be served with all the conditions desired so that the *naos* will be able to navigate for the ports which Your Highness decides upon and [that] they will go securely without receiving any hindrance. All I desire is as Your Highness will desire and have, which is, moreover, your service.

"Your Highness will know that all your *naos* that arrive here, to them I give all the provisions and the things which were required by them of me. And they proceed upon land securely, as in your land, and Your Highness will be more assured by them of this, and of my will, for the great desire I have for your friendship.

"Very powerful lord, so that Your Highness will be more entirely assured of our great love, I dispatched this letter, for by it we will be able to know the will of Your Highness, not desiring another thing than the great friendship of Your Highness, as you will wish with true peace which is good and a blessing, for which I ask that you give all dispatch to the reply of this letter, as a lord of such great power; we await it, because in it is all our hope, and seeing it, we will remain more secure and with very great pleasure, and we do not have a greater care in the heart, than the reply of this letter, which we pray that it is as we hope. All these things Your Highness will have for certain and we ask you to provide us with certainty and with friendship and affection, guarded among us forever."

Cartas dos Vice-reis: Documento Número 108
of the Torre do Tombo

PORTUGUESE TEXT

E todo meu querer e deseyo e meu bem poderoso Rey de Portugall senhor justiçoso senhor da terra e do maar Rey nomeado por todas as partes do mumdo em crispãos na Persya na Arabia nomeado e avido por senhor de gramde poder com ajuda do Senhor e senhor de gramde sabedoria com gramde famaa e de todos bemquisto por suas hobras

Sabera vosa Alteza mujto poderoso senhor que hum capitam vosso veyo a hum porto que esta jumto com esta çidade de Bemgala chamado aque cama dom Joam com quatro naos e mamdou hũu batel a esta cydade omde eu estou com gramde amizade a qual muyto tempo avia que desejaua e folguey muyto com elle polas nouas por que tamto avia que esperaua loguo lhe ofereçy todo meu poder e a çidade e o que lhe comprise que fose seruiço de vosa alteza pella qual rezam ficamos muyto amygos com gramde vomtade do que algũ tamto fico reçeoso ate ver çerteza de vosa alteza

Sabera vossa alteza que veyo Joanes feytor a hum porto perto desta çidade de Bemgala chamado Quylaa o qual veyo em huũa não da terra com huũ mercador della e huũ Fernamdo e me derom huũa carta de seguramça e eu não quys comfiar e aquyxera mamdar a dom Joam por que não ey de comfiar ate nom ver a vomtade de vossa alteza/

fol 1v Sabera vosa alteza que eu não quero maays daquilo que vosa alteza for seruido com toda a comdiçam que quiser por que as nãos posam navegar polos portos como vosa alteza detrimina e amdem seguras sem lhes ser feito nenhuũ noyo tudo quero que seja como vosa alteza quiser e ouuer que seja mays seu seruyço

Sabera vosa alteza que todas as naos suas que aquy chegam lhes dou todos os mamtimemtos e as cousas que per eles m'eram requerjdas e amdam na terra seguros como na sua

142

e vosa alteza podera ser mais çerteficado deles disto e da vomtade que lhe tenho polo gramde deseyo que tenho de sua
amizade

Muyto poderoso senhor pera que vosa alteza fose mays em-
teiramemte çerteficado de noso gramde deseyo mamdey
esta carta pera por ela sabermos a vomtade de vosa alteza
nom desejamdo outra cousa mays que ha amyzade gramde de
vosa alteza como quiser com verdadeira paaz bem e bem pello
qual lhe peço que a reposta desta carta nos mamde çedo
como de senhor de tam gramde poder se espera por que nela
esta toda nosa esperamça e vemdo a ficaremos mays seguros
e com grandisymo prazer e nam trazemos outro cuydado
mayor no coraçam que a reposta desta carta a qual pedimos
que seya como esperamos Isto tudo tenha vosa alteza por
çerto e lhe pedimos que nos proueya com çerteza e com
amyzade e bem queremça a qual seja guardada amtre nos
pera sempre

TABLE OF CONTENTS

PART I

EMBASSIES, NAVIGATIONS AND PEREGRINATIONS

CHAPTER I. THE KINGDOM OF CAMBAY

144

PART II

DESCRIPTIONS

145

APPENDIX

INDEX

INDEX

Barbudo, João, 80

Barbudo, Tristão, 69, 72, 74-76, 98

Barcunda, See Bihar

Baroda, 13, 29, 119

Barreto, Diogo, 11

Barriga, Alvaro Lopes, See Lopes, Alvaro

Barros, João de, 3, 8, 9, 11-19, 21, 22, 24, 25, 27, 29, 30, 32, 35, 36, 39, 41, 45, 47, 52, 54, 56, 61-64, 67-72, 74-81, 83, 99, 100, 104, 115, 126, 127, 132

Bayley, Sir Edward Clive, 14, 25, 30, 40

Beja, Diogo Fernandes de, 41-44, 46-48, 50-57, 61-63, 66

Beja, Jorge Barreto de, 61

Belem, 71, 140

Bengal, 30, 54, 66, 67, 69-72, 75-81, 83-89, 92-96, 98-101, 126-130, 132-135, 137, 138, 141

Bengal, Bay of, 78, 98, 100, 101, 126, 130

Bengalis, 70, 72, 73, 75, 81, 82, 86, 128, 129, 137

Benjamin, 31

Berbera, 67, 117

Berredo, Francisco Pereira de, 21, 22, 24, 27

Bhagua, 53

Bhatkal, 21, 30, 117

Bihar, 126, 127, 137

Bihar Khan, See Muhammad, Sultan

Black Tomas, 21, 22, 25

Blochmann, H., 83, 85, 128

Bogra, 137, 138

Bombay, 16, 17, 53, 66

Brahmans, 12, 23, 42, 46, 47, 109, 110, 112, 113

Brahmaputra River, 128, 137

Brava, 117

Brazilwood, 117

Brema Limma, 126

Briggs, John, 14, 40

Brito, Antonio de, 80, 81, 84, 85, 92, 93, 95, 96, 100, 137

Brito, Christovão de, 32, 57, 58

Brito, João de, 32

Brito, Ruy de, 67, 68

Brito, Simão de, 80

Broach, 53, 116

Bulnei, 127

Burhanpur, 118

Burma, 70, 98

Cabral, Pedro Alvares, 8, 9, 115

Cairo, 41

Caixa, See Kai Shah

Calicos, 118

Calicut, 9, 10

Cambay, 8, 10-14, 16-18, 21-44, 46, 47, 50-55, 61-66, 69, 96, 102-104, 106-110, 115, 117-120, 122, 124, 127, 130, 131, 138, 140

Cambay, City of, 8, 37, 105, 109, 113, 115, 118, 119

Cambay, Gulf of, 12, 22, 66, 104, 105, 109, 113, 116

Cambayet, See Cambay, City of

Camelo, Fernão, 63

Cananor, 16, 19, 21, 26, 27, 32-37, 40, 41, 67, 68

Caor, 128

Caor River, See the Brahmaputra River

Carnelians, 57, 58, 114, 138

Cassius Dio, 55

Castanheda, Fernão Lopes de, 3, 8, 9, 11, 13, 14, 17-19, 21-25, 27, 30, 35, 36, 39, 41-49, 52, 54-56, 61, 63, 64, 69-78, 96, 98, 100, 133

Castelo Branco, João Gonçalves de, 61

Castile, 9

Catechu, 31

Ceylon, 30, 69, 78, 99, 101, 102, 130

Champanel, See Champaner

Champaner, 13, 23, 24, 28, 38, 39, 44, 46, 47, 55, 62, 66, 115, 116, 119, 120

Chanderi, 39

Chatigam, See Chittagong

Chaul, 11, 12, 36, 37, 39, 42, 57, 58, 63, 104, 117, 118, 127

Chaul, Battle of, 12, 16

Chaul, River of, 99

INDEX

INDEX

INDEX

INDEX

INDEX

INDEX